QUICK SEX, SLOW DEATH

Kendall Francois's fingers closed around the prostitute's throat like a vise. Startled, she grabbed for them and began struggling. But it was no contest. The petite woman was no match for the six-foot-four, 380-pound ex-wrestler. He squeezed harder, determined to kill her. He twisted around and brought the woman's body down to the bed, still holding hard to her throat. Her struggles became weaker. Then it was over. Francios's powerful hands had strangled the life from his newest victim.

He took the body into the bathroom and washed it clean in the tub. Then he slung it over his shoulder and headed for the attic to dump it with the other bodies. He noticed it was getting a little crowded. He'd have to move the body to the basement tomorrow; there was plenty of room down there. Enough for this body . . . and the bodies to come.

Other Books by Fred Rosen

NEEDLE WORK
BLOOD CRIMES
DOCTORS FROM HELL
LOBSTER BOY
THE MAD CHOPPER*
DEACON OF DEATH

Published by Pinnacle Books

*written under the name Kent Allard

BODY DUMP

Fred Rosen

PINNACLE BOOKS
Kensington Publishing Corp.

http://www.kensingtonbooks.com

Some names have been changed to protect the privacy of individuals connected to this story.

PINNACLE BOOKS are published by

Kensington Publishing Corp.
850 Third Avenue
New York, NY 10022

All Kensington Titles, Imprints, and Distributed Lines are available at special quantity discounts for bulk purchases for sales promotion, premiums, fund-raising, and educational or institutional use. Special book excerpts or customized printings can also be created to fit specific needs. For details, write or phone the office of the Kensington special sales manager: Kensington Publishing Corp., 850 Third Avenue, New York, NY 10022, attn: Special Sales Department, Phone: 1-800-221-2647.

Pinnacle and the P logo Reg. U.S. Pat. & TM Off.

First Printing: July 2002
10 9 8 7 6 5 4 3 2 1

Printed in the United States of America

For my dear Aunt Irene and Uncle Nat

Prologue

September 1998

Eight women were missing. Only he knew how many more he had eliminated.

Eliminated. That was a good word to describe what he did. Once he was through with them, the women ceased to exist; he just . . . *eliminated* them.

To their grieving families who couldn't find them, they vanished off the face of the earth. To Bill Siegrist, lieutenant of detectives dedicated to tracking him down, the harsh fact that his victims were prostitutes worked in the bad guy's favor.

Prostitutes, Siegrist knew, followed a nomadic lifestyle. One day they were working Main Street, the next Oak Street, the next . . . who knew? They might find a sugar daddy who would take them off the street and support them. Or maybe they would escape from the city's cold and damp into the warmth of Florida or California or Arizona.

Street people. They vanished without a trace.

The majority of the time, it was not murder, just a by-product of their lifestyle. Nothing for anyone to worry about, in fact, maybe even a good thing. The more hookers that got off the streets, the less the cops had to run them in for prostitution. That meant less of a strain on the legal system and less for the reformers to kick up a storm about.

Eight prostitutes in a city of just over 28,000, a city where everyone knew everybody. The cops knew the prostitutes and the prostitutes knew the storekeepers whose stores they stood in front of, trying to attract the men in their cars to pull over to the side of the street and ask them to hop in. The storekeepers up and down Main Street knew the eight who had vanished off their street in the downtown area of the city. So, where were they? A few blocks away was the answer.

The house looked like something out of a Vincent Price movie. It was an old Victorian that children walking by could easily fantasize was haunted. But they had to walk fast.

"The place smelled something awful," said Jim White, the postman who had the house on his regular route. "But I couldn't figure out what it smelled from. It was just awful."

People would gaze up at the gables of the old Victorian, wondering what in hell that smell was. At the Arlington Middle School where one of the residents worked as a hall monitor, the kids noticed the odor emanating from him and *they* wondered what it was.

It was a stink reeking off his massive, wrestler's body, the kind of body capable of putting a man in a stranglehold that would quickly leave him unconscious. The kids had coined a name for the hall monitor that would dog him for the rest of his life.

Stinky. The kids had called him Stinky.

So he smelled; so do a lot of people. But Stinky smelled from body odor and something else. That "something else" was hard to define. Only a war veteran would have known what it was. It was a smell etched in memory, created in battle. The odor never faded from consciousness. It was a simple smell, actually, an elemental smell, as elemental as life itself.

It was death. That was what he smelled of. Death.

PART ONE
The
Serial Killer

One

Highland is a pleasant small town on the west bank of the Hudson River. Located just one mile from the Mid Hudson Bridge, the town lies in a narrow valley that provides picture-postcard, Norman Rockwell winter scenes of snow-covered hills and kids on sleds going down steep slopes during the winter months.

In the summer, the town transforms itself from its sleepy winter hibernation into a tourist spot of antiques stores and hole-in-the-wall restaurant finds. Still, unless one is a shopkeeper or restaurateur, making a living can be tough.

Route 9W, a long state highway that stretches from the New York City border north to Albany, meanders through Highland's outskirts. In the summer, chili cook-offs, crafts fairs and country festivals can be found in back of the churches and schools that border the road. In the fall, pumpkin festivals are held in the large fields scattered along this 150-mile stretch of four-lane blacktop.

At various points along the way are independently run motels, the kind that have long since been passed by the major chains because 9W is no longer a main thoroughfare. That distinction belongs to the New York State Thruway, Interstate 87, to the west. Still, if a cheap, clean room with few amenities is wanted, a motel on 9W is a good bet. The Valley Rest Motel was one such place. Like most, it had been built in a u-shape. Wendy Meyers had taken up residence in one of the Valley Rest's rooms. The place wasn't expensive, so it was affordable to a street person like Meyers. A small, slight woman, Meyers was thirty years old. Her mug shot, taken after an earlier arrest for prostitution, shows a woman with dark eyes, high cheekbones that could have belonged to a model, a long aquiline nose and a jaw that jutted out almost defiantly. By the time she walked out of the Valley Rest Motel on Route 9W in Highland on October 24, she had more than her fair share of responsibilities.

Besides her relationship with her boyfriend, Meyers had a son who lived with his father in Ayden, South Carolina, the man Meyers had married and subsequently divorced.

Wendy Meyers had been born in the nearby town of Carmel, and given her mother's name, while her brother George bore their dad's name. A second brother had been named Albert. The men had moved to the warmer climes of Bell, Florida.

It probably came as a surprise to some people that Meyers was a member of St. James the

Apostle Roman Catholic Church in Carmel, given her profession. She was a prostitute. She had turned to prostitution to support her burgeoning drug habit.

Prostitution is a business requiring the right business climate, that is "johns." Highland is small and doesn't have enough trade. People also talk. Women like Wendy Meyers, who had had a life in front of them that had turned downward to drug hell, found that the only way to support their habit was prostitution. The only place in the vicinity that had a lot of men willing to pay for sex was the big metropolis across the Mid Hudson Bridge—the city of Poughkeepsie.

With all its economic travails, Poughkeepsie was a busy place and so was the Mid Hudson Bridge. More than twelve million vehicles a year use the bridge. Most come from the rural hamlets on the other side of the river. Highland is one such place, a bright, happy, sunny place with a stream flowing directly through the town. It is the last place a murder trail would be expected to begin from.

Wendy Meyers hitched the last ride of her life. As the car she was in crossed the river, Meyers was actually looking up at something really special. The Mid Hudson Bridge has often been recognized by bridge-building architects and bridge aficionados as one of the most beautiful suspension bridges in the world.

At the ribbon-cutting ceremony on August 25, 1930, New York State's first lady Eleanor Roosevelt stood in for her husband, Franklin, the state's governor and future President. When the ribbon was cut, traffic began pouring over the 3,000-foot span almost immediately.

On the other side of the bridge, the driver let Meyers off on Church Street. Thirty years before, when Lieutenant Bill Siegrist had been a raw twenty-two-year-old recruit assigned to foot patrol, Church Street was just a narrow block, with room for only one car to pass at a time. Set at the curbside were neat two- and four-family houses and occasional stores.

As the 1970's progressed and urban decay set in, Church Street was literally thrown down and widened. It was transformed into the street with main access to the bridge to expedite traffic through the city. Siegrist could understand the need to do that, but he also felt that the city lost some of its charm with those changes, not to mention the human toll. Residents were forced to sell out and move someplace else.

To stimulate the city's economy, a downtown civic center was built beside a Sheraton Hotel. The idea was to attract major conventions. It did, in a limited way, though not enough to revive the town. Conventions, plus the occasional "knife show," touring circuses and music acts, did bring some additional revenue into the area. The Bardovan Theatre, which was built in 1869, was even restored to its former glory.

Despite such civic improvements, the town's economy still floundered and the city and the surrounding township, which contained 42,000 residents, fell further into the economic doldrums. What kept the city afloat was IBM, which had a major plant in the town and supplied a good portion of the city's tax base. But Wendy Meyers wasn't in the least interested in IBM, or what the city would do if the techno giant gave the city the old heave-ho.

Wendy Meyers walked over to the mall, right off Main Street. Back in the 1980's, the place was a big hangout for school kids and people who just wanted to go shopping at one of the outdoor mall's many stores. There was a place where kids could buy jeans at good prices, a fish market, which always had fresh catches, and the tuxedo store where kids went to pick up their tuxedos for the high school prom. But as the 1980's wound into the 1990's, urban blight set in.

The kids stopped hanging out at the mall because it was too dangerous. Drug addicts and prostitutes began to clog up the place. Sometimes there would be fights, shootings—it definitely wasn't a good place for good people to hang out at or shop, anymore.

Meyers passed the mall and stood on the corner of Jewitt Avenue where it crosses Main Street. It was a good place to pick up johns, with lots of traffic. After a few minutes of waiting, she got her first bite when Kendall Francois, driving his 1984 red Subaru, pulled over to the curb.

Francois remembered her from a previous occasion. He recalled that she had ripped him off. She had, according to his memory, taken his money, but had not given him enough sex in return.

Francois opened the window. They began haggling about price and when they finally settled on one, Meyers got in on the passenger side and Francois drove off. He tooled his car smoothly through Poughkeepsie's streets, observing every traffic law, neither going too fast nor too slow, nothing to attract attention.

When he got to his house a few blocks off Main Street, he parked in his driveway and escorted Meyers upstairs to his second-floor bedroom. Like most prostitutes, Meyers was smart enough to demand payment up front. With johns you never knew. They could always try to stiff you.

Francois took out a wad of bills and paid her. It was time to go at it.

She pulled her pants and panties off and Francois took out his penis. There were no pleasantries, no romantic idyll and no foreplay. Just straightforward intercourse. He got on top of her and began pounding inside her. It must have hurt to have him doing that, not just from the force of his member but from the sheer weight of him on top of her. Meyers was a slight girl. It probably felt like she couldn't breathe.

It's unclear exactly what she next said, but Francois would later recall it as something like "I've had enough!" or "Look, I, uh, have another appointment I have to run to." It is also unclear what, if any, change took over Francois's face and/or body when the big man went from being just an abusive john to a serial killer.

Did his expression turn from a snarl into rage? Did it look like another personality had taken over? No one knows. He did, however, say in his later statement to police that he was thinking something like *How dare this whore try to stop me? How dare she not give me what I paid for?*

Wendy Meyers would be his first "kill."

Hands that had once, with ease, pushed back three-hundred-pound opposing wrestlers in high school, closed around the throat of Wendy Meyers. Hard. Harder. Harder still. You have to have strong hands and squeeze awfully hard to strangle a person to death. For Meyers, the pain would have been the least of her problems.

Francois was literally choking the life out of her. She would have been conscious and known what was going on for at least the first minute and a half. Then mercifully, her brain reeling from oxygen deprivation, she would have blacked out. Until then, it would be sheer, un-relenting agony.

Even when she went limp in Francois's hands, he would know she was unconscious but not dead. If he stopped strangling her, it was possible she could be revived. But Francois kept strangling her until he heard her hyoid, or throat bone crack, and added still more pres-sure until she was clearly, definitely, absolutely dead. Releasing his grip, she would have fallen to the floor.

It was a beautiful late autumn day, the tem-perature in the mid-seventies. Francois could hear the traffic sounds from Main Street, sounds drifting genially in on the wind. He could hear the songs of the birds that congregated in the trees in back of his house.

Silently, Francois picked up the body. He carried it into the second-floor bathroom. He placed Meyers in the bathtub and turned on the faucet. Slowly, almost reverently, he placed her in the water. It was almost as though he wanted to make her clean for her passage into the next life.

When he was satisfied that she was clean enough, he took her out, dried her off and then placed her on his shoulder. On the second-floor landing, he opened a door set into the wall. A stairway led upward to the attic.

Francois carried the body up the stairs and into the attic. He placed it in a black, plastic garbage bag that he'd brought with him, the super-duper size normally used to haul leaves. Then he closed the bag over her head and placed the sack deep into the large, stuffy room. If his parents or sister or anyone came up to look, all they would see was a big bag filled with . . . whatever.

His work finished, Kendall Francois walked down the stairs. It was still the middle of the day and he had plenty of things to do.

October 26, 1996

After two days, Wendy Meyers's boyfriend reported her missing to the Town of Lloyd police.

Highland was in the town of Lloyd and since that was where she was last seen, they had venue.

Immediately, the town and city of Poughkeepsie police departments were notified that a Missing Person's report on a Highland resident, Wendy Meyers had been filed.

"Her boyfriend was a suspect," Bill Siegrist recalled. "[They were] hot on him."

But after Meyers's boyfriend submitted to a polygraph and passed, he was crossed off the list. As for the involvement of City of Poughkeepsie detectives, it wasn't their investigation. When a person is reported missing to the police department of Highland, there is not much Poughkeepsie, despite its close proximity, can do. If Poughkeepsie got a lead that the missing person was somewhere within its borders, they could move in. Until then, the investigation lay with the town across the river.

Police entered Wendy Meyers's name in the computer. It was actually not a bad place to be for a missing person. The New York State Police maintains a central database that every police department in the state has access to. The New York State Police Management Information Network (MIN) Missing Persons File lists every missing person for whom a report has been filed.

Every year, 35,000 people are reported missing. And every year about 31,000 show up, a phenomenal recovery rate of 85 percent. The other 4,000, or 15 percent, are still listed as "missing."

Among other fields that data entry clerks fill in are the circumstances surrounding the person's disappearance and the location where he was last seen. Those two factors are all important in solving a single homicide, let alone a string of them. But prostitutes are different from "normal" civilians. The assumption the police made was that Wendy Meyers was a street person and subject to a street person's vagaries of life.

Prostitutes lead dangerous, unstable, dysfunctional lives. Meyers was not some middle-class housewife with regular habits. Her disappearance was most probably due to someone who was keeping her. Maybe she'd gone to Florida without telling her boyfriend. Who knew?

Or maybe she had gone down to New York City to go shopping. She'd probably turn up like most of the other 35,000. There was no reason to suspect she had been abducted or, worse, murdered. Maybe it would have helped if the cops could have seen Meyers differently, as a girl who started out with real dreams that were thwarted by a drug habit she had to feed and a life of prostitution to pay for it.

Maybe, maybe, maybe.

While the cops hoped Wendy Meyers would soon turn up, she lay in her makeshift, last resting place. She was inside a middle-class house on a tree-lined street, just waiting for somebody to figure out where she was.

Albany, New York

For twenty-seven years, Senior Investigator James "Jimmy" Ayling had been a New York state trooper. He began his career in central New York, where he eventually rose to the rank of sergeant. Modeled along military lines, with ranks from trooper through colonel, the state police was a great place for an enterprising young guy like Ayling. After a few years on the force, he became station commander in the Oneonta barracks. While he was climbing the ladder, Jimmy Ayling had time to get his Bachelor of Science in criminal justice.

Ayling doesn't look like a cop. With a shocking head of carefully combed, thick, gray hair, he seems more like a corporate executive. In a sense, that is one of the roles of his job, making sense out of and leading a corporate hierarchy. But the one he leads is not charged with ruthless business dealings, but with saving lives.

Tall and well built, though thickening a little with middle age, Jimmy Ayling is the senior investigator in the New York State Violent Crime Analysis Unit (ViCAP). Previously known as Homicide Assessment and Lead Tracking (HALT), ViCAP was created to help police officers around the state identify and apprehend serial killers, rapists and other violent offenders.

Under the State of New York Executive Law, 221-B, "Every law enforcement agency which received a report of an actual or attempted abduction or molestation shall notify the New York State Violent Crime Analysis Program (ViCAP) via the requirements of the New York Statewide police information network of such report. Such program shall make comparisons of data in its files and report to the law enforcement agency making an initial report any similarities to other reports received by such program. The Violent Crime Analysis Program shall also notify the unit of law enforcement agency which investigates homicides when a report reveals similarities, patterns or modus operandi which appear in reports of homicides."

"New York State ViCAP serves as a central contact point and resources for all law enforcement agencies to assist in the investigation of violent crimes," explained Ayling.

Having the information to catch the bad guys is dependent on all police agencies in the state providing ViCAP with information on crimes, especially the ones that are unsolved. That means someone actually has to sit down and enter that information into the database.

The program itself provides the following:

- Searches for case similarities to link or match cases and/or offenders submitted by different agencies;
- Cross-searches for similarities between cases in different categories, e.g., missing persons and homicide;
- Comparisons and searches of the Abduction/Molestation File for similarities;
- Time lines for potential or suspected serial predators.

Ayling's second-floor office is cluttered and the clutter makes it look smaller than it is. On the walls are quotations he has saved over the years, poems and commentary about the policeman's lot. There is no missing the huge, twenty-one-inch computer screen that dominates the room.

Every day, Ayling comes in and quickly scans the New York State Police Management Information Network (MIN) Missing Persons File for anything unusual. When he saw that Wendy Meyers's name had just been added, he didn't pay any more attention to it than any other name. Or any less.

No one knew that a serial killer was swimming around like a shark in their midst. Like that predator, the serial killer lurks and waits to pounce, many times at the weakest link in the chain, on the edges of the circle. And that's exactly what prostitutes were, street people who existed on the edges. But not in Poughkeepsie.

As much as the city protested, it was not one at all. Poughkeepsie was really a small town posing as a city. Everyone knew everyone else, and that included the prostitutes. They would be missed.

If someone requested his help, Ayling could be helpful. But before beginning a ViCAP investigation, there has to be a crime. Simply being missing is not a crime, unless there is hard evidence of foul play. More important, for a homicide to be investigated, a body is usually needed. Someone has to be dead in a way that is not consistent with natural causes. Minus that, all the computers, manpower and brainpower in the world are powerless. Someone has to initially put together that a number of missing people could be the result of an unknown party killing them.

Considering the good odds that most missing persons turn up intact and well, the criminal perpetrator who decides to commit serial murder, and hide the bodies, gets a tremendous edge. He may continue to kill until such time, if at all, that his crimes are detected. Sometimes, serial killers actually get away with it. Jack the Ripper is the prime example.

November 29, 1996

Twenty-eight years old, Gina Barone was born in Yonkers, New York. Her parents moved to Poughkeepsie when she was a child.

"I went to school with Gina Barone," said Mike Grimley, a construction worker. He was speaking in the Eveready Diner. The Eveready is right on Route 9 in Hyde Park, less than a mile from the city of Poughkeepsie.

"Gina was a nice girl," Mike remembered. "I spent many an hour with her, just laughing and having a good time."

That was before Barone turned to drugs and then to the street to support her habit. Over the years, Gina had had one child, Nicole Renee. Barone's drug habit had become the most defining relationship in her life. The only way to support it was to take to the streets and reel in as many johns as she could. It was during that second part of her life, when she became a street person, that she made the acquaintance of Kendall Francois. Kendall Francois and Gina Barone had "dated" on more than one occasion. He was one of her cash-paying customers.

Gina Barone had a nice smile, even in the mug shot taken after being arrested on a prostitution charge. She was the kind of girl Francois liked—white, with a full head of brown hair and a petite body. Like many in her generation, she found tattoos attractive. She'd had an eagle tattooed on her lower back. More noticeable was the "tat" on her right arm, the letters "POP."

The night of November 29, Gina Barone had an argument with her boyfriend, Byron Kenilworth. He left her in the area of Academy and Church streets. She had on a pair of jeans and a close-fitting shirt meant to show off her slim figure. Barone decided to pick up some money by "working" Academy Street. Shortly after she began displaying her body for business, a familiar two-door 1984 red Subaru pulled over to the curb near where she was walking.

It was up to the customer to say what he wanted. For her to do so in advance was to invite an arrest on a prostitution warrant. It was never clear who might be a police informer, so it was always a good idea to let the john name what he wanted. Make the customer do all the talking. If the suggestion came from the customer, there was no crime until a price was negotiated. By that time, most girls had had enough of a chance to smell out the john and make sure he wasn't a cop.

In Kendall Francois's case, that was probably impossible, considering he stank to high heaven. Unless he was paying, no woman would want to be in the same room with him, let alone have him put his "johnson" up her "jackson." They negotiated a price for straight "69." From past experience, Barone would have known that was Francois's favorite.

Gina Barone suggested a place off Route 9 to do it. Francois must have agreed that was a good place because that was exactly where he drove. For some reason, he wasn't anxious to get home. Maybe he was contemplating what to do, or maybe he just wanted a change of venue. Whatever the reason, it was eleven P.M. by Francois's reckoning as they drove through the city's deserted streets. There was a chill in the air; winter was coming very soon. The town just hoped it wouldn't get hit with a cold winter, which would be made even worse by wind whipping in across the Hudson River.

From where they parked the car on a side street off Route 9, they could see the river, all black and silent, its current flowing south toward New York City. Barone might have glanced out the window at the river, or the deserted highway, but she was a good business-woman—she most definitely would ask him for money before they did anything. Then it would have been time to face what all the girls knew about Kendall.

Two

The girls had talked about it over and over. None of them enjoyed sex with Kendall Francois; he was just too damn large. But he paid, and that was all that was important to an addict: getting enough green to buy the drug of choice, then move on to the next customer, a never-ending cycle of physical and financial abuse.

After the sex, Francois would later say Gina Barone asked him for her money. He would remember thinking, *I've been ripped off.* It must have been hard for Barone to understand what he was pissed about. The guy just seemed to suddenly fly off the handle because he didn't think he'd gotten his money's worth. Could he have misunderstood that he was to pay one hundred dollars for sex and thought it'd be less?

Francois continued to complain to her that she had not given him the sex he was paying hard cash for. Gina Barone must have been perplexed. They had had sex; it didn't make any sense. Suddenly, a strong pair of hands wrapped themselves around Barone's throat. She might have reached up to try to fight him off, but that would have been futile. What could she do? She was an out-of-shape 110 pounds to his stocky, powerful 380.

Her strength would have begun to fade in direct correlation to the oxygen being deprived to her brain. Soon, her hands would have fallen limply to her sides, her eyes gazing out on the world for the last time and then, finally closing.

They were still in the car parked on a side road. It was quiet, the clock approaching eleven-thirty P.M. Looking out, Francois saw nothing—no stranger, no car, no cop, no street person, no anything. Nothing unusual happened in the area where he had just killed Gina Barone that would make police take notice. Francois had just done what every bad guy aspires to: he had committed the perfect crime. He had killed a prostitute who he figured wouldn't be missed with nary a witness in sight to ID him or his car. The only problem, of course, was getting rid of the body.

Pushing her down under the seat so she wouldn't be seen, Francois drove his car the few miles back to his house and parked it in the garage in back. When he got out, he looked around to make sure no one was out and about in the neighborhood. He needn't have worried; no one ever was. If anyone ever looked out back to see what he was doing, they kept their presence quiet.

Francois reached back into the car and pulled the limp form of Gina Barone out and into his arms. It was dark outside, not much light, and he didn't feel like stumbling around in the dark with a body. If he should trip on anything and the body fell, then he would have to collect her up again, and that was a quick way to be seen. Such an eventuality was best avoided.

Francois decided to leave her in the garage. The next morning, when no one was around, he'd move Barone up to the attic. The dead woman was placed on the cold concrete floor of the garage for temporary storage. Then Francois went into the house and up to bed, where he slept soundly.

In the morning, when Francois came out, Barone was still there. Not that he expected she would be gone. He knew she was as dead as a doornail, but it was good to have it confirmed one more time. Reaching down, he picked her up. She was as light as a feather. Taking careful looks at the houses next door and all around him, he saw that no one was out at this early hour. He couldn't see behind closed curtains, but he assumed no one was there watching.

Carrying her in his arms, he smuggled the body into the house. Then it was up the stairs, and up farther still to the attic. He put down Barone's body and placed it in a large, black plastic bag. Trash bag. That was what she was to him—trash. Something to stuff into a bag and get rid of.

Francois pulled the ends of the bag together and tied them loosely. He had to admire the construction; the bag hadn't even ripped. Then he pushed her back into the attic into a prone position. He looked down at the trash bag, making sure it was where he wanted it. Satisfied, he climbed down the attic stairs.

At the bottom, he pushed the door closed. Just a door like any other door. Nothing suspicious about it. He went back downstairs in time for breakfast as though nothing unusual had happened. As far as he was concerned, things were normal, including the bodies he was storing in the attic.

Cathy Marsh was all of four pounds when she was born on a cold winter morning, in the Upstate New York town of Schenectady. It was a really bleak place then, before the Capital Region's buildup in the 1970's. The Capital Region encompassed Albany, New York's state capital, and the surrounding cities of Rensselaer and Schenectady.

After her birth, Cathy's parents, Marguerite and James Marsh, watched as their youngest daughter was put into an incubator that was necessary for her survival. Her survival was by no means certain.

"She was a very small child, very tiny," said Jordan Baker, a family friend. But Cathy survived. "Cathy had a little pixie haircut back in those days, a real short haircut. When she went to the store, they used to think she was a little boy," continued Baker. "Cathy developed into a feisty kid. She set [people] straight."

Like any kid, Cathy sometimes got in over her head. There was the time she was only a few years old and she was playing. She tripped and broke her leg. It was a compound fracture and the doctor made a cast for her from the toes to the waist. Cathy survived this accident and continued to grow and get strong.

A few years later, tragedy struck when Cathy's father, James, principal of the John Bigsbee Elementary School in the Mohonasen School District, died when she was eight. But she still had her mother, her older sister, Ruth, and older brother, Robert.

By the time she got to high school, she had matured into an athlete, with a short, stocky frame. Her dark blond hair trailing after her, she would race down the wooden floor of the gymnasium at Mohonasen High School, calling the plays as one of the school basketball team's two guards, the shortest positions on a basketball team.

At other times of the year, she played on the girls' softball team. She had a deft, determined way of running the bases, and surprising power from someone so small. Intellectually, her teachers thought she had the promise of a college career in front of her.

Her family happily snapped pictures of her at graduation. Then, after graduation, there was that day in 1986, when she, her sister, Ruth, and her brother, Robert, and some friends hit the road to Myrtle Beach, South Carolina, to celebrate their freedom from the confines of adolescence. Everything was in front of them. They were now adults with a boundless future.

Many kids in such small communities wind

up going to local community colleges. Some take required liberal arts courses before transferring to a four-year school. Others decide on the two-year associate's degree and take practical courses in subjects like criminal justice. They become cops or prison guards. Others opt for an easier way to make money, taking courses like "Computer Information Systems," frequently a way to get hired by IBM.

Contrast that with a kid who shows some promise and opts for, and is accepted into, a state university. With its high academic requirements, the four-year SUNY College at Binghamton is the crown jewel in the statewide system of four-year colleges. But there are other four-year state schools to attend if you don't have the grades.

Cathy Marsh did not have the grades to attend Binghamton. Nevertheless, her grade point average and SAT scores were high enough to meet the SAT and GPA cutoffs at the State University of New York at Geneseo. Marsh got to Geneseo by going west on the New York State Thruway. She passed through farmland that was rich looking and fertile in the late summer sun, arriving in Geneseo, in the far western part of the state, in late August 1986, for the beginning of the fall 1986 semester.

According to the *New York Times,* Geneseo has become "one of the country's most highly regarded public colleges." The school has been consistently ranked among the nation's top colleges in annual guides published by *U.S. News*

& World Report, Time and *Money* magazines. The school's on-line catalogue breaks down its information in the following way: Academics; Access Opportunity Program; Applying to Geneseo; Visiting Geneseo; Orientation; Campus Map; Tuition/Fees; Financial Aid; Scholarships; College Offices; About Geneseo; Life on Campus; Athletics; Campus News; Calendar of Events; and Technology Resources.

While universities and colleges must, by federal statute, make public crimes that are committed on their campuses, they are under no obligation to indicate to students if there are any problems with drugs. The schools are trying to attract students or their parents, who are usually paying all or part of their expenses, by emphasizing the positive aspects of campus life.

It was during her first year at Geneseo that Cathy Marsh began using cocaine on a regular basis. How much she had done before, if any, is open to conjecture. What isn't, according to later published reports, is that Cathy Marsh became a cocaine addict sometime during the 1986–1987 academic year. Her sister, Ruth, would later write:

"Cocaine took your life before this day/always hanging on when you tried to get away."

For Catherine Marsh, the 1980's would flee into the 1990's like some long, wet, humid night. It eventually ended, for a while, when she left college and came home to Schenectady. The grit Cathy had brought with her into life, that helped her survive her sickly birth, that was responsible for her athletic triumphs, she brought to her struggle with drug addiction.

This time, she lost.

According to police records, Catherine Marsh was arrested on misdemeanor prostitution and drug charges in Syracuse, on a number of occasions. She had probably picked Syracuse, as opposed to Schenectady, as the place to prostitute herself for her habit because Syracuse is fifty miles from Schenectady and no one knew her there.

In New York's small, upstate towns, people talk. They gossip. Neighbors that seem at first blush to be friendly are actually the types who traffic in other people's problems. By traveling to another city to exercise her criminal career, Cathy was saving herself the derision of her hometown.

Somewhere in the middle of her headlong gallop to throw her life down the drain, Cathy had time for some brief relationships with men. From those relationships came two daughters, Erin and Grace. And still, despite their love, and her family's support, Cathy drifted further and further down into the drug culture.

In 1995, Cathy managed with one last, desperate effort to take control of her life and tried to salvage what was left. Making the greatest sacrifice any woman can make, she allowed her children to be adopted. In so doing, she acknowledged that another woman would make a better mother than she was. Cathy then traveled south to Poughkeepsie, where she entered a drug clinic. She hoped the therapy she received there would save her life.

Addicts during rehab regularly attend twelve-step meetings, where they acknowledge their powerlessness over their substance abuse and come to believe that a power greater than themselves can restore them to wholeness. Essentially, they are accepting their addiction and realizing they have no control over it. Recovery requires a series of progressive steps where the addicted individual agrees to make amends to those he has harmed because of his addiction, all the while leading a sober life.

Catherine worked her program of recovery diligently. She had a sponsor to support her. She began keeping a diary of her feelings, which is always recommended to recovering addicts. In it, she wrote how, at times, she was disappointed in herself for failing her friends, including occasionally missing her regular twelve-step recovery meetings.

She began taking classes at Dutchess County Community College. Her identification picture from there shows a chubby-faced woman with a long jaw leading up to a prominent nose, close-set blue eyes and a carelessly chopped pageboy haircut. She is smiling. It was a good pose, a sober pose. But her addiction was always there, lurking in the background, very sly, just waiting to take hold again.

When addicts falls off the wagon, the time they have in rehabilitation does not mean they start the addiction phase from scratch. They return to the addict's life at the point where they were before they got into rehab. If, before rehab, you were looking over an abyss ready to jump, you go back to that hell.

Despite her best efforts to work her program, Cathy felt she needed coke to survive. She was desperate to plug up this hole inside herself and the drug could do that, at least temporarily, from fix to fix. Only the drug would do. What pushed Cathy off the wagon is unclear, but fall she did. The inevitable question confronted Cathy again: how to pay for the addiction? Cathy had no money. She could go to her family. But what could she say if she did?

"Hi, Mom, please give me some money to buy the drug that's killing me."

That wasn't realistic. The alternative was clear. She turned to the streets again to support her habit. Again and again, when she needed a fix, she went to the street to pick up guys. There was one charge for giving head, another for a full "69." Men liked her; she had no problem getting business.

Kendall Francois was a repeat customer.

November 31, 1996

How many men who were the picture of normalcy drove north on Route 9 on their way to work and gazed to the left at Marist College, evaluating the school's security? Actually, the place had no security to speak of. The campus gates had no guard posts. Anyone could get in at any hour.

Fronting Route 9, not more than a few hundred feet from the road, but still on campus, were garden apartments where some of the coeds lived. Francois could see the kids going to and from class in front of these dorms. The place looked, and was, almost all white. There were a few people of color. If he went on campus, he would easily be taken for an older student, or a laborer. The girls were certainly pretty.

They had young, taut, white bodies. He could fuck them like they'd never had it and then bring his hands up around their necks and squeeze. He'd feel the adrenaline rush as he crushed their necks in his hands, bare of gloves, wires, or any sort of strangling implement.

He liked the feel of skin on skin. It gave him sexual power. But that was all dependent on the girls being his type. Sadly, the Marist coeds— well, they were attractive, he wanted them, but not enough to "do" it. Then he thought about the women at the end of his block.

The block he lived on was Fulton Avenue. It might have been an avenue in the last century, but now it was just a narrow street. Walking out the front door of his house and turning left, a few hundred yards down at the end of his block was another campus. This one was full of even snootier white girls, but no less pretty. The place was called Vassar College. Formerly an all-girls' school, it had long since become coed. Still, the place was known for the refined beauty of its female population.

Francois liked looking at the girls. But "doing" it to them? It was sexual power that he craved, power and control. Something inside, that instinct for survival that the best jungle animals have, that told them which were the weak ones in the herd to pick on and which were the strong ones, told him that the coeds were too strong.

Besides, they weren't street people. Their relatives and friends would know they were missing and come looking for them. He needed women who were more . . . anonymous, compliant, controllable, who would do what he wanted. But definitely white girls.

In matters of lust, Kendall Francois shunned his own race. Kendall Francois just loved white girls. They had to have a particular body type—small of frame, with thin, sometimes emaciated bodies. And they had to be impure; women of low self-esteem, desperate women who didn't mind his body odor and sold their bodies to the highest bidder in order to get money for a fix.

The women Francois craved most were white prostitutes. Like his English predecessor that the press had named "Saucy Jack," forever more known by his more popular name, "Jack the Ripper," he was attracted to prostitutes. There were a few girls in town who met his criteria. They weren't expensive to have. What he liked to do was have them over to his house. When his mother wasn't there.

Kendall looked over at his mother beside him on the car seat. Like the dutiful son he was, Kendall Francois was driving her to work at the Hudson River Psychiatric Hospital, located on Route 9, right at the edge of the city's boundary. A series of low-lying, institutional-looking, brick buildings scattered on carefully manicured grounds, it was there that Francois's mother, Paulette, worked as a psychiatric nurse.

That morning, like many others, Francois drove his mother up the hospital's winding driveway and dropped her at the entrance. After exchanging "have a good day" pleasantries, he drove back down to the road and took a left.

Passing Marist College, he couldn't help a sidelong glance at the attractive women roaming the campus. He continued driving past the shopping center on his left, until the four-lane road became a highway within the city limits. Traffic speeded up. As the road came within the downtown section of the city, it widened into two fast lanes in each direction with one, main interchange near the center of the city. The sign to the exit on the left said CHURCH STREET. Francois took it and headed his Subaru around a sharp left curve that brought him back onto the same road, Route 9, only this time going north. It was confusing to out-of-towners, to have to go north in order to get off the highway from the south side. But Francois, being a local, was very used to Poughkeepsie's vagaries.

Still going north, he stayed in the left lane and went up the ramp labeled CHURCH STREET. The ramp climbed over and across the highway. It let him off onto Church Street, the four-lane, one-way street that looked more like a boulevard than a street.

Francois took a left and began zigzagging his way through the side streets. Finally, he came out on his favorite haunt, Main Street. He tooled his car down the two-lane blacktop, looking out the window at the fast food restaurants lining both sides, mixed in with pawnshops, groceries and dry-cleaning stores.

It was late fall and there was a real chill in the air. If this was fall, winter was going to be a lot worse than anyone thought. The Hudson Valley had a tendency to see temperatures plunge in January and February. Even those who liked cold weather didn't look forward to the cold snaps. However, the cold was good for something: it slowed down decomposition.

Francois slowed down as he approached the intersection of Cannon Street with Reservoir Square. Looking out the windshield, he spotted her at the curb. He remembered her from their other times together. Her name was Cathy. There were a few other women out there, too, like that girl Cheryl, he'd also had, but for some reason that day—it really wasn't important why to him—he wanted Cathy. She met his criteria; she was white and thin and a warm body to be abused.

Francois pulled over and glided to a stop. He reached and opened the passenger-side window. Cathy looked over and saw it was Francois. She knew he stank. But his money was good and she needed it soon, and bad. They negotiated the price for intercourse. Soon, they agreed on a number and Kendall opened the passenger-side door.

From past experience, Catherine Marsh knew that Kendall Francois liked to fuck at the big man's house. She wouldn't have been surprised, then, that he drove over to his house, parked in the garage out back, then walked the few steps from the garage through the back door of the house, then up the stairs, to his second-floor bedroom. Cathy followed him.

Kendall's room was a mess of filth. There was underwear strewn about the room, some of it smelling from strange pieces of a brown *something*. Cathy either held her breath against the stench or just took it and rationalized that it wouldn't take long for her to make the money.

Francois passed over some bills. Cathy would probably have counted them up quickly and when she was sure she wasn't being cheated, begin to undress. Francois would have gotten on top and pounded his penis inside her as hard as he could. Francois would later say that he suddenly became enraged.

"You cunt!" Francois shouted.

He shouted some more obscenities. He was still in her when he began to squeeze her throat with his powerful hands.

Three

Whether she fought or not is unclear, but knowing how hard she had fought to start her life, there is no reason to assume Cathy Marsh fought any less hard to stay alive. She would have summoned up all the strength she had built up over the years as an athlete. But much of that was gone. It had disappeared with her lifestyle. The addiction had sapped her of everything, including her life.

Francois kept squeezing and heard a dull crack, the breaking of the hyoid bone. After a few more minutes, Francois was satisfied that Cathy Marsh was dead. He released his grip and she collapsed to the floor. Outside, he could hear the traffic and the wind. Inside, he heard nothing, save for his own breathing. He lifted the body off the floor and took it into the bathroom where he placed it in the tub. He turned on the water and bathed the dead woman and then later removed her to the attic.

He threw Cathy Marsh in beside them. Wendy Meyers and Gina Barone now had company. He could tell from the stink that the first two were well on their way through decomposition. Still, they didn't smell as bad as they might have because of the cold weather. Francois was storing the bodies in the attic, which was normally a place without proper ventilation. It kept in heat in the summer, cold in winter. If the weather continued to stay cold, the bodies wouldn't rot as fast and smell as much.

He closed the door to the attic and went down the stairs and back into the bathroom, where he washed his hands carefully and dried them. Then he went back downstairs and outside to his car.

It was cold, yes, but a nice day. A very nice day.

December 9, 1996

Patricia Barone was worried. She knew about her daughter's lifestyle, but it was unusual for her to lose contact for a prolonged period. She always kept in touch. Her boyfriend had told her about their argument, but that wouldn't account for her daughter's sudden disappearance. With a creeping dread filling her heart, the type of anxiety that any mother would feel when her child was missing, she called the police on December 9 to report her daughter officially missing.

"If you have a routine, most normal people check in at various places throughout the day. If they don't show up, people think there's something wrong. But with a street person, they have no normal routine. They have no sched-

ule. There's no one there to backtrack from,"
said Bill Siegrist. By 1996, Siegrist had worked
his way up the Poughkeepsie Police Department ladder and become a lieutenant of detectives.

"Street people have no concept of time and
locality because their life revolves around making money to get drugs. That complete involvement. If not for Gina's mom reporting her
missing, no one may have. It's essentially a cold
trail."

It is a public misconception that random
murder is more frequent that it is. When someone disappears and foul play is suspected, those
closest to the missing person are always suspected first. Most murderers know their victims.
It was only logical that when the City of
Poughkeepsie Police Department picked up the
cold trail, they suspected someone close to
Gina: her boyfriend, Byron Kenilworth.

If Siegrist had a nickel for all the times a
relative who had reported a loved one missing
turned out to have murdered that relation,
he'd be rich. Kenilworth was the logical suspect. It was only logical then, that the cops suspected the boyfriend, Byron Kenilworth. It
would be a lucky break if this case fit the pattern. Then there'd be no need for further investigation.

Cops depend on certain things in their investigation of crime, not the least of which is
the lie detector. Despite the fact that it can't
be used as evidence, cops have so much confidence in the machines that they regularly use

them to rule out suspects in homicide cases. The first to take a polygraph in the Barone case was Kenilworth. He had agreed to take a lie detector test to prove he was not a suspect.

A polygraph, or lie detector as it's commonly called, is actually a series of measurements taken in response to a series of questions. Pneumographic tubes measure respiration. There are two plates that record galvanic skin responses. A blood pressure cuff records relative blood pressure and pulse. Essentially, what the specially trained lie detector operator has done is tap into the body's autonomic nervous system, whose activity an individual has no control over. Questions that make them want to lie create an emergency to their psychological well-being. This fear of detection causes the sympathetic branch of the autonomic nervous system to react. That reaction produces palpable, recordable changes in the nervous system. Those changes signal deception. At least, that's what the police think.

In their heart of hearts, cops believe no one can lie to and beat a polygraph test. They have to believe that because they rely on them. In most instances, they're right. But there are the rare times when the person sitting in the chair can lie about an event and the machine will not record that lie. Instead, their responses are recorded as truth.

According to the *Diagnostic and Statistical Manual of Mental Disorders (DSM)*, the standard diagnostic textbook among psychiatric professionals published by the American Psychiatric

Association, someone suffering from dissociative amnesia, for example, would have "an inability to recall important personal information, usually of traumatic or stressful nature, that is too extensive to be explained by normal forgetfulness."

Therefore, if the killer simply blocked out the event in his mind and forgot about it, and was subsequently asked about it during a polygraph, his response that he didn't kill someone, even though he had, would be correct because he had forgotten about it. His response would be measured as truthful by the test.

Or, a person might be suffering from schizophrenia, which the *DSM* defines as "a mixture of characteristic signs and symptoms. . . . that have been present for a significant portion of time. . . . These signs and symptoms are associated with marked social or occupational dysfunction.

"While the diagnosis should always be by a trained medical professional, if an individual has trouble keeping a job, having relationships, plus has hallucinations, feels they have to give in to some irresistible impulse, such as to kill, a positive diagnosis for this disorder can be made."

In such an individual, there would be no feeling of guilt when a criminal act was committed because the act itself isn't real. It's part and parcel of the psychosis. Such an individual would have no problem beating the lie detector.

"When was the last time you saw Gina

Barone?" the polygraph examiner asked Kenilworth.

"The night before she disappeared," he answered.

"Did you have an argument?"

"Yes."

He had previously admitted that to police, but they wanted the question put to him while hooked up to the machine.

"Have you seen her since?"

"No."

"Did you have anything to do with her disappearance?"

This was a very important question. In the case of Susan Smith, she had told the nationwide media that her missing children had been kidnapped. The nation bought her story, which, as it later turned out, was false. She had drowned them in order to take up with a rich and handsome man.

"No," Kenilworth answered. He'd had nothing to do with Cathy's mysterious disappearance.

"Do you know anyone who had anything to do with her disappearance?"

"No."

The test over, Kenilworth was allowed to cool his heels while the operator went over the results and consulted with detectives. It didn't take long for the operator to determine that all the squiggles that had shown up as a result of the questioning proved decisively that Byron Kenilworth had had nothing to do with his girlfriend's disappearance.

Byron Kenilworth was what he seemed—an anxious and worried stricken boyfriend. He had passed the lie detector test with flying colors. The following day, December 10, was Gina's twenty-ninth birthday. Unless she suddenly reappeared, it didn't look like she would be around to celebrate it.

January 4, 1997

It was an absolutely ugly, low-lying building. Everybody in Poughkeepsie knew it as the headquarters of the Poughkeepsie Police Department. As you walked in the lobby there was a reminder of times past, the old green globe that had adorned the doorway of the old precinct. The globe had been lovingly restored to its former glory.

Next to the globe were letters in gold leaf spelling out CITY OF POUGHKEEPSIE POLICE DEPARTMENT. The letters had adorned the door of the old police station, too. Like the globe, the letters had been restored and repainted to their former glory. History was important to the Poughkeepsie Police Department.

The detective division was in the back of the building. The lieutenant of the squad shared a narrow, fifteen-by-fifteen-foot office with his sergeant, Raymond Horgan. Bill Siegrist remembered when he had been the sergeant. That had been in the early 1990's, when he had been promoted to detective sergeant and transferred to the detective bureau. But that hadn't lasted long. His record was so good in the detective bureau that he was needed elsewhere.

On November 15, 1995, he was promoted to lieutenant and went back to patrol as the head of that unit. Then, once again, the department needed his help, which was how Bill Siegrist found himself transferred back to the detective division as the lieutenant in charge.

He noticed, as he looked around, that his office still had blue walls, battered tan filing cabinets and two institutional-style desks. The lighting was overhead fluorescents that gave everything a washed-out, yellowish tint. Siegrist looked around the room again. He had to smile. It had taken him a mere twenty-eight years to get this promotion.

Bill Siegrist always wore distinguished-looking gray suits that made him look more like a banker than a cop. The tip-off to who he was, besides the gun he wore clipped to his belt that was hidden by his suit jacket, was the way he walked. Siegrist still maintained the quick gait of the beat cop he would always be in his soul. New times, though, demanded new methods.

Siegrist had a computer to build his databases. He could access it at any time to get background information on any suspect. Still, he had come up the old way and preferred more of the old-fashioned methods.

Back in 1993, he and another detective had gone down to Baltimore on a case. They spent some time with the homicide squad profiled in Paul Attanasio's book *Homicide,* which became the basis for a critically acclaimed television series. It was while he was visiting Baltimore Homicide that Siegrist noticed the board on the squadroom wall. Reproduced on the television show, it lists homicides according to the following criteria: "victim"; "detective assigned to the case"; "prosecuting DA"; and "case number."

Siegrist liked that way of cataloguing homicides so much, he imported it to his new assignment with the detective division. The Poughkeepsie board, like that in Baltimore, listed all homicides in the city with the names of all cleared or solved cases in black, while unsolved cases were in blue. His group of twenty detectives handled all the felony investigations in the city of 24,000.

Neither Wendy Meyers nor Gina Barone was on the board. They were officially classified as "Missing persons." Siegrist knew that most missing persons turned up alive. No one had yet reported Catherine Marsh missing.

"Prostitutes are picked on like garbage," says Siegrist. "They are the hidden society on our streets, the hidden victims. Nobody pays attention to her. If a prostitute's missing, nobody can give you an accurate date and time that they were missing because they move around so much. Conversely, people who engage in a lifestyle of drugs and prostitution have no sense of time. Their whole life is built around their next fix."

Which was a more detailed explanation as to why the missing women were not on the homicide board. Maybe they had gone someplace else, some other city to get money for their next fix. Maybe they had decided, hopefully, to get out of the racket. Maybe they had kicked their habit.

Maybe, maybe, maybe. The bottom line was the police knew they were missing, but without a crime or a crime scene, without a *body*, what could they do except file the report in their computers and hope for the best?

Wendy Meyers's boyfriend suspected foul play and decided to act on his suspicions. He came to the Poughkeepsie Police Department to ask for their help in tracking down his girlfriend.

"He'd been in trouble before," Siegrist recalled, "and knew all the guys in the detective division at the time. And everyone knew Wendy, too."

Siegrist turned to Detective Skip Mannain for help.

Karl "Skip" Mannain was the grandson of Irish immigrants. His father had been a firefighter. Mannain could recall a fire that burned the belongings of a family with ten children. His dad had collected clothing and furnishings to help the family out. Mannain himself had followed through on that caring tradition.

A Mexican immigrant named Jaime Gil had died in a hit-and-run accident. After apprehending the driver, Mannain had searched Gil's room for information on his next of kin.

He found a stack of letters from the man's family back in Pueblo Nuevo, Oaxaca, Mexico.

With no money to ship the body back home, Mannain took up a collection. When he was finished, he not only had enough to send the man home and have him buried, but there was money left over to help out his widow and children. The disappearances of the Poughkeepsie prostitutes appeared to be, at least on the surface, a lot more complicated.

"What's going on with Gina and Wendy?" Siegrist asked Mannain.

"Wendy's boyfriend is asking us for help in finding her," Mannain answered.

"There's a million places she could be. Gina, too."

Siegrist went back and checked the Missing Person's report on Meyers. He had Mannain canvass the streetwalkers. They had absolutely no idea of the whereabouts of the missing women.

"I say to have one person missing from a location for an extended period of time is unusual," regardless of their occupation. "To have two, especially two who live the same life, that is a very unusual event. Both women had gone through Thanksgiving, Christmas and New Year's. They had not contacted their family or friends. It was the beginning of a new year and there was no trace of them," said Siegrist.

He felt something was not right.

"Right from the very beginning, I had a deep concern about what happened to these women.

In my heart, I know people come to Poughkeepsie to buy prostitutes and drugs."

That means the city attracts some pretty unsavory characters, characters who think nothing of committing violence in pursuit of their goals.

"It's pretty elementary stuff. You don't have to be a rocket scientist to figure it out," Siegrist said matter-of-factly.

Siegrist was being polite. What he really meant to say was that there was a load of scumbags, liars, cutthroats, cheats and murderers working Poughkeepsie's streets. Any one of them could have killed the missing women.

Four

January 13, 1997

It was cold, too cold really to be a hooker on the streets of Poughkeepsie. With the wind chill factored in, the temperature hovered around zero for many days. Inside his Subaru, Francois never felt the cold. He kept the heater on; he was comfortable. But not the women. His women.

Prostitutes advertised their wares, their bodies. It wouldn't do if the johns couldn't at least get a limited view of what they were paying for. Thus, in the middle of winter, women with short skirts and wearing high heels could occasionally be seen on Main Street. As long as the snow did not overwhelm the sidewalk, they were there. As were the johns.

The johns cruised up and down the street, carefully looking at the women. Not all men, of course, were cruising for women. Some even failed to actually see the women. For these men, not attracted to the seamy underside, it was almost as though the prostitutes blended into the landscape, however garish or unusual their dress. This was, after all, New York State, where the unusual was not considered out of the norm.

The women who plied their trade in the shadows of Main Street knew something was wrong. They talked amongst themselves about it, careful to share any information about abusive johns. They tried not to get into cars with men they did not know, but that was impossible a lot of the time. When they needed a fix, they needed a fix; only money would do. Still, they talked.

What had happened to Gina, Wendy, Catherine and now Kathleen?

Kathleen was Kathleen Hurley. As of yesterday, she, too, was missing. She was nowhere to be found—not in her apartment, not on the street, not anywhere. Like the others, she had just disappeared.

The women on the street expected the worst. How could they not? They knew that some john was preying on them. Why else had the girls just suddenly disappeared? Maybe the cops bought the "I'm moving on to a better place" scenario; the girls knew better.

They were dead. In any empty lot or maybe dumped in one of the area's many lakes. The girls depended on the cops to catch the guy. But despite the danger they were obviously in, they couldn't help law enforcement. There was a natural antagonism between the two groups.

Cops arrested prostitutes for what amounted to a victimless crime, then forced them to hire attorneys with their hard-earned money. That was the reason they sold their bodies—the money. And to have to spend it on anything other than creature comforts, like to pay some lawyer to keep them out of jail for soliciting, well, that was just too much. Besides, the prostitutes figured the cops didn't care about them. That was why nothing had really been done, they felt, to find the missing girls.

Detectives from Siegrist's detective squad, led by Skip Mannain, hit the streets to try to get the girls to talk with them. At first, they were reluctant to say anything. They also didn't want to be seen by their clients as stool pigeons. If any of the more violent johns found out they'd been informed on, they'd beat the shit out of them. Or worse. And hang what the cops said about protection. A girl's got to make a living, right? And she can't do it in protective custody, right?

Gradually, though, a growing sense of unease, of real foreboding, hit the women. Reality was inevitable. Either they talked and took the chance the cops might actually find someone responsible for the disappearances or they kept their mouths shut and continued to play Russian roulette with every john. Finally, some girls began talking.

It was just a little at first. Then, more. Siegrist began to get a feel for the street and the dangerous lives these women led. Names began to come out, names of the men who were considered abusive to the women. The cops were able to make a list of the names of the few johns who liked to get rough. The list would be checked out.

In his office, Siegrist glanced to his right at the big, dry-erase board that listed the names of all murders in Poughkeepsie since 1993. The names Wendy Meyers and Gina Barone were not there. Yet.

January 15, 1997

Kathleen Hurley had been gone for three days when her family reported her missing.

Like the others, Kathleen Hurley was white, had a small build and brown hair. She had a noticeable tattoo on her left bicep, the letters "CJ" imprinted on the skin. Her mug shot, taken on the occasion of an arrest on November 11, 1987, showed a dark-haired woman with wide-set, rheumy-looking eyes, pursed, thin lips and a strong jaw. At the time of her disappearance, her family said in their report, she was forty-seven years old.

The cops, of course, were the last ones to know she was missing. They always are. First her friends on the street knew she was gone, then her family and then, finally, the police. Siegrist looked at the Missing Person's report. Siegrist saw that Kathleen Hurley had had lesbian lovers.

"She'd had a fight with one she was living with. Kathleen had left their apartment and never showed up again. She left all of her stuff and never came back."

If she had found a better gig someplace else, didn't it make sense that she would at least take her personal belongings? The same thing with the other girls: not one of the first two reported missing had taken anything of personal value along with them into the ether. The logical supposition, then, was that Hurley had hit the streets to pay for drugs. But why hadn't she returned?

"I was convinced something wasn't kosher," Siegrist explained. "That was three girls we knew of who'd disappeared. Something had happened to these girls."

He assigned Mannain to do the usual canvass. Mannain went out on the street and asked questions of Hurley's associates. It was a dead end. No one had seen anything, no one had heard anything, and no one *did* anything. Mannain, of course, was frustrated. He suspected foul play, but he couldn't prove it. Once again, no crime scene, no victim, hell, no criminal. The girl had vanished, just like the others, completely eliminated.

The cops began seriously wondering now. After getting past the obtuse possibility that all four women were now living the Life of Riley on some beach somewhere, they came to the inescapable conclusion that someone had eliminated them. But who? And how? Siegrist began looking for a pattern. The Poughkeepsie Police Department needed the help of their next-door brethren.

"Skip and I went to the Town of Poughkeepsie Police," Siegrist recalled. " 'Here's what we have,' I told them and gave them the names of the missing women and the circumstances of their disappearances. Maybe some of what happened to these women [foul play] happened in the town of Poughkeepsie.

"I knew there was a question in their [Town of Poughkeepsie Police] mind, that these guys think I'd just taken command. But they know [from past experience] I'm pretty accurate."

The Town of Poughkeepsie Police could add nothing that was helpful in finding the missing women. Siegrist was once again left to conduct the investigation on his own.

February 1997

Francois drove slowly down the street in his red Subaru, looking for his next victim. Then he saw her. She was white, 5'4" and weighed 110. When he pulled over to the curb next to her and rolled down the window, the girl looked in. She had brown eyes and brown hair and something else—a one-inch scar on her left cheek. How she had gotten it, Francois didn't know. It was obvious from her profession that she didn't have the money to pay for plastic surgery, unless she started charging a thousand a trick, which, of course, she would never get.

The girl, thirty-one years old, was Mary Healey Giaccone. She had previously been convicted of misdemeanor prostitution. She was a "pro." Francois and the woman stood there on the street for a moment negotiating a price for sex. When they were both satisfied and the bar-

gain was made, Giaccone got in and Francois
drove off. It was the last drive Mary Healey
Giaccone would ever take. Less than an hour
later, she lay with the others.

March 7, 1997

After six weeks of not hearing from her,
Catherine Marsh was finally reported missing
by her mother.

"When's the last time you saw Catherine?"
Skip Mannain asked her.

Her mother, Marguerite, replied that the last
time she talked to her daughter was November
11. The cop then asked her the usual series of
questions cops ask in missing person's cases:
did she have any enemies?; did she know of
anyone who would want to hurt her?; any idea
where she might be?; any idea who she might
be with? The answer to all the questions was a
resounding "no."

It was damn frustrating! The cops wanted to
do their job and find the girl. Revise that: girls.
With Marsh, the total of missing women the
police knew of was up to four. No one had seen
anything; no one knew anything. Mannain tried
backtracking Marsh's movements from the day
she disappeared, but it was impossible. So
much time had passed, the trail wasn't cold, it
was Arctic. Permafrost covered it.

"She was involved in drugs?" Siegrist asked.

"Right," Mannain agreed. "And prostitution."

But if Marsh had found herself and gone into drug rehab, would she then suddenly have left the one thing that was bringing her salvation? If, however, she had found a way to do that with good reason, wouldn't she have let her mother, to whom she was close, know what was going on? The answer was unfortunately "yes," which left the idea of foul play a distinct one.

What Siegrist and Mannain didn't know, though, of course, now suspected, was that Catherine Marsh had been murdered. There were four missing Poughkeepsie women. They had to admit the possibility, the distinct possibility, that they had a serial killer in their midst. Siegrist agonized about what to do.

The lieutenant reasoned that they could go public. It was hard to tell how the citizens of Poughkeepsie would react when they found out that four women had disappeared and that police feared the worst. There was a good possibility it would only serve to scare and worry the populace without producing one lead. The other possibility was to keep investigating without warning the public of the suspected killer in their midst.

In the end, the decision was made to quietly continue the investigation, but with more manpower. The public, however, would know nothing about it. Despite the fact that the disappearances of all four women was a matter of public record—Missing Person's reports are public documents—the local paper, the *Poughkeepsie Journal,* did not pick up on the story. It was really just a country paper with big-city pretensions. The other newspapers that served the city, the *Middletown Herald Record*, the *Daily Freeman* and the weekly *Poughkeepsie Beat*, all failed, too, to see the emerging pattern.

To Kendall Francois, it was all a mystery. He didn't realize he had killed five women. When he looked in his attic, he was surprised to see five bodies instead of four. How had the fifth gotten there? He remembered Giaccone, but not Hurley.

Someplace, deep down in his mind, he had a dim recollection of strangling Hurley. Who she was and how he had come to pick her up, he just didn't remember. But it didn't make a difference. It was just one more body to decompose in the silent graves he had given them all in the attic.

Bill Siegrist sat in his car down by the water. He looked out at the Hudson River. He came down to the deserted waterfront park many times in the course of the week just to think.

He lived only eight miles out of the city in a town called Pleasant Valley. And it really was that, a direct bucolic counterpart to Poughkeepsie's urban chaos. Just miles away was the twenty-six-year-old house he lived in with his wife and kids. It was a nice house, a beautiful house, but there was a problem.

The roof was getting old. It really needed to be replaced. There were other improvements on the home that he also wanted to make, but he was too busy to do any of them. He never seemed to have the time. Time and again, he'd been home doing something of importance for his family when he got a page to come in. If a major case was breaking, he had to go—heck, he *wanted* to go. Still, what a pain it sometimes was being a cop.

Siegrist munched on his sandwich. He drank his coffee. He became aware of the silence, broken only by the police scanner on the floor that he kept perpetually on, in case he was called. He looked out at the gulls flying over the bridge. He tried to play out a "what if" scenario—what if the women had been killed? The killer would probably have dumped their bodies.

Siegrist had had his detectives search some of the more remote wooded sections of town. All they found was snow and, under that, just the frozen ground of the Hudson Valley. Siegrist then sent Mannain out again on the street to interview the streetwalkers with a different question.

"Who's weird?" Mannain asked the women.

The girls, knowing they had a killer preying on them, finally opened up. They named the weird johns. Those names were added to the previous list of the abusive ones. The cops were constantly busy checking out all the leads.

Siegrist took a bite out of his sandwich and slugged it down with hot coffee. He turned the defroster on to clear his window of the fog. As it worked its magic and the windshield became clear, Siegrist looked up at the majestic river materializing in the autumn sunshine. Siegrist pulled out a copy of a report Mannain had filed. In it, the detective had detailed his findings. The prostitutes said there was this guy.

"What guy?" Mannain had asked.

"A fat guy," they said. "A big guy."

"What about him?"

"He liked to choke some of the girls."

"This big fat guy have a name?" asked Mannain.

"Francois," the women answered. "Kendall Francois."

Siegrist started up his car and drove up the hill and back to his office, parking in the lot behind the station reserved for police officers. He strode purposefully into the building, passing the old police globe and the newly restored letters spelling out the constabulary's formal name.

Once he was in his office, Siegrist looked up Francois in the computer. Maybe the guy had some sort of record involving force or even sexual crimes. That would make him a suspect worth looking at further. He got a hit almost immediately.

Earlier in the year, Francois had solicited sex from an undercover cop. He was arrested. Francois had pleaded guilty to criminal solicitation, a misdemeanor, received a fine and no time.

What Siegrist did not know was that in the course of his employment applications with both the Arlington Middle School and the Andersen School, Francois had filled out forms that asked him if he had ever been convicted of a crime. In each case, he had checked the box that said "no."

Neither school checked to make sure he was telling the truth. If the Andersen School had, since Francois had started there after his conviction, it would have discovered his record. That a man convicted of a crime involving sex could teach, or be around children, was unconscionable, but the truth was no one had violated the law.

For over twenty years, a state law that required criminal background checks of all employees had protected New York City schoolchildren. Poughkeepsie had no such law. Many in the community wanted it, but for various political reasons, it had never been put on the books.

Siegrist knew that lots of guys solicit sex and most of them are definitely nothing more than lonely guys who can't get a woman unless they pay for her. Except for that one conviction, which was pleaded out, Kendall Francois didn't have so much else as a parking ticket. There certainly was no record of brutality. In some quarters, he might be viewed as a model citizen.

Model citizen. Somewhere on his desk, Siegrist found it, Cathy Marsh's Missing Person's file. He began rifling through it. He kept turning pages until he found it, the one item that had struck him when he looked at it before. It was under "Background."

Before she disappeared, Cathy Marsh had gone for some prenatal counseling. The missing woman was pregnant with her third child when the fiend, whoever he was, had killed her.

Five

Bill Siegrist had managed to maintain a low profile for most of his career. He wasn't a flashy cop who grabbed headlines, and was more prone to giving the credit to the guys who worked under him. He was very happy when Skip Mannain got the story about his involvement in the case of the Mexican immigrant in the *Reader's Digest*. In the early part of his career, Siegrist had managed to make it into the national press, too.

It was during the Tawana Brawley case, when the Reverend Al Sharpton came up to Poughkeepsie to stage a demonstration against what Sharpton perceived was the police force's "racism." One of the demonstrators got unruly enough that Siegrist had to put a chokehold on the guy to contain him. A photographer took the shot, which went out over the wires. Soon, Siegrist was being held up in the national media as an example of the Poughkeepsie cops' racism.

Siegrist had, in fact, done nothing wrong. He had acted well within his authority as a peace officer to quell a potential riot situation. After Sharpton left to take up some other cause, Siegrist's notoriety faded. As it did, he began to climb the police force's corporate ladder. As his fortunes rose, the city's continued to fade.

By the early 1990's, IBM had hit a dry spell. A combination of declining sales, subsequent layoffs and reassignment of personnel to other plants shortened the revenue stream. That left the town dependent on the monies brought in by students for a revenue source.

Vassar College is located in the town of Poughkeepsie, Marist College in the city of Poughkeepsie. Both are four-year schools and students continue to come and spend their money in the town. Still, the combined enrollment of both schools is 20,000, hardly enough to keep the local economy flourishing.

The city and the town overlap and in most instances, it makes no difference where you are—same diners, same mall, same gas stations. But the police forces are different, which makes it easier to commit a crime and get lost in the bureaucratic confusion.

Every day on his way to work, Kendall L. Francois made a right turn onto Route 9 in Poughkeepsie. Poughkeepsie is a city in the middle. Ninety miles south is New York City; seventy-five miles north is the state capital of Albany. Locals like to describe themselves as living in the Lower Hudson Valley.

As he tooled his two-door red 1984 Subaru up the suburban highway, on his left Francois passed Marist College. The coeds at Marist came from the rural towns of New York, New Jersey and New England where the biggest urban problem was winter snow removal.

Marist had originally been founded by the Marist Brothers order and while it no longer was under church control, it still maintained close enough affiliation with the church that many concerned parents felt it safe to send their sheltered children to the school. Some coeds had been educated at strict Catholic schools where the Catholic Church's edict was the rule of law, none being more important than the Fifth Commandment, "Thou shalt not kill."

Once in a while in their hometown, there might be a murder, the type of thing where some woman gets liquored up, then catches hubby with another woman. Or another man. Or maybe the sexes were reversed. No matter. It all fell under "crimes of passion." Such things did not happen to "good" girls.

Murder happened to the other girl, the one who hadn't kept her nose clean, who went out with the exciting boy from the other side of the thruway. The thruway was the region's major traffic artery, the route most of the women traveled to Marist.

When they got to Poughkeepsie, there was a lack of realization that they were in an urban environment with a high crime rate. Some women forgot to lock their doors. The Marist women were incredibly naive. For Kendall Francois, they were potential prey.

Located on Route 9 in the town of

Staatsburg, a short, twenty-minute ride north of Poughkeepsie, is another institution of learning. Called the Andersen School, it is a private facility for the mentally retarded and other developmentally disabled children. The mission of the Andersen School, as stated on its Web site, is "To always put the student first, and to provide functional and educational opportunities to achieve quality of life outcomes for children and adults with autism or other developmental disabilities."

The core values of the school are to enhance the quality of life educational opportunities, to treat their children and adults with dignity and to demonstrate respect for the interests, abilities, values and needs of their people.

Evidently, Kendall Francois reflected these values because the school had hired him. A man who clearly appreciated education, Francois both worked as a professional in an educational environment and took classes. In 1994, Kendall Francois enrolled at Dutchess County Community College, where he loved to play cards, usually Spades.

"I played cards with Kendall a lot," said Marion Ross. "He never liked to lose, but if he lost, he was okay with it. He was the nicest guy."

His government studies professor at Dutchess was Richard Reitano.

"He was a good student, not a great student," Reitano would later say in a local paper. "He participated in class, had a good relationship with me and the other students and seemed to really get something out of the classes. He had an appropriate sense of humor, a good understanding of government, and he spoke very eloquently at times on the rights of African Americans. He was a picture of normalcy."

His house definitely was not. With its scabrous, decaying appearance, the place looked eerie even to those who didn't believe in bogeymen.

The first mention of the house in official records was October 1, 1869. On that date, the deed changed hands between the original owner, William H. Worrall, who had died, and Peter N. Howard, who bought it.

By January 20, 1975, when Kendall Francois's parents, McKinley H. Francois and Paulette R. Francois, bought it, the house had changed hands a total of only three times in the previous 106 years. It still stood in a stable, solidly middle-class area. Except for the new, paved road, the neighborhood had changed little in the intervening years except, perhaps, for one thing: the Vassar Garden Apartments.

They were decidedly lower-class garden apartments at the end of the block. To move from there into one of the block's one-family houses would be to "arrive." That was exactly what the Francois family did in 1975, when they bought William H. Worrall's house on Fulton Avenue.

The place needed a lot of work. Beams on the lower level were exposed. The paint was chipped, the beautiful Victorian details of the house, in the molding and on the walls, in the woodwork of the banisters, floors and doors, all had been lost over the years to layers of paint and plaster and apathy.

The Francois family probably did their best to keep up the house and it really shouldn't have been a hard job. The whole house measured less than fifteen hundred square feet. Paulette and McKinley were full-time working parents, with four kids to raise and support. Over the years, the maintenance of the house and the grounds, a little yard out back and a porch with a small sloping lawn to the street out front, had gone by the wayside. Walking by it and looking up, the house looked as though it was decaying.

By 1996, Kierstyn, the youngest, was still at home. Francois's older sister, Raquelle, lived someplace else in Poughkeepsie. His kid brother Aubrey also did not live at home.

Kendall Francois was born in Poughkeepsie on a hot summer day, July 26, 1971. The New York State Department of Health does not allow public access to birth certificates, so it's unclear how big a baby Francois was at birth. But even as a child, his girth began to be noticed by the other kids in the Vassar Garden Apartments.

Neighborhood children used to taunt the fat, black child about his weight in that "Nah nah nah nah nahhhh nah" singsong children's cadence. And he wasn't happy about it. Mark Gehringer, a fellow who knew him as a child, said that the neighborhood kids "would yell out to him 'How now, brown cow?' and he used to get upset."

"He kept to himself," growing up, another friend from his childhood recalled. "The people around here keep to themselves."

Which was why later, when the house on Fulton Avenue started to smell, the neighbors said and did nothing. Maybe they whispered amongst themselves. Poughkeepsie, though, was a conservative place. What someone did in the sanctity of his or her home was no one else's business.

By high school, Selma Darrell remembers, Kendall Francois had become an average student.

"I was his high school French teacher," Darrell said. "He seemed to be gentle."

A gentle giant. Darrell took a liking to the big kid.

"He tried to work for me [at school jobs] with limited success."

Francois seemed to be one of those students of limited intellectual ability. He sat in the back, hoping he wouldn't be seen or called on. Darrell, a pro, saw what he was doing and intervened.

"I actually put him in front of me to help him," she recalled.

Maybe by being in front of the teacher he'd absorb more and get his grades up. But it didn't work. Francois soon realized that there was "safety" in being seen, that the teacher would call on the kids in back who seemed to be hiding instead. In Francois's case, it worked because, "He did not talk a lot," nor did Darrell call on him frequently.

"He was barely an average student," she remembers.

It was that "averageness" that hid the terrible rage building up inside.

Francois's tenure in Arlington High School lasted from 1984 to 1989. During that time, Darrell recalled, "The black kids in Arlington stuck together. There weren't many in class." But there did not appear to be the overt isolationism seen by minorities in other communities. Oliver Mackson, who attended Arlington High School and later became a reporter for the *Times Herald Record* newspaper, remembers things a little differently.

"Arlington was a comfortable place for lots of different crowds. Even runty, dorky, mouthy Jewish kids like me got along fine with all kinds of people," he would later write in his column of June 23, 2000.

One of Mackson's friends, he wrote, was Ross Allison, who was a good enough wrestler at Arlington to wrestle in state tournaments. After graduating in 1982, he continued his participation in the sport by refereeing wrestling matches.

"Sometimes, when I was not refereeing, I would go to a home Arlington match. He'd [Francois] be there with his father; they'd be standing in the corner and I'd go say, 'Hi,' " Allison recalled.

Maybe it was a way to get out the aggression that had been building inside him. Or maybe he just wanted to fit in. Whatever it was, Francois decided to use his bulk for his own benefit.

Kendall tried out for and immediately got on both the football and wrestling teams in his freshman year. He was all of fourteen years old. By the next year, he had physically matured to an almost muscular 6'4" and 250 pounds. But he still had this baby fat that he seemed desperate to get rid of.

In the team wrestling photo of that year, Francois stands off at the side of the photograph, the last of nine wrestlers, the only one wearing a cut-off jersey, deliberately doing a bodybuilder's side chest pose. The pose is meant to show off the pectoral and bicep muscles. He still had the fat, but his chest was huge. The expression on his face was one of challenge.

That same year, "He broke his hand doing something stupid," Allison remembered.

Francois had had an argument with another kid and broke his hand. That kept him out of wrestling for the year, but not football. Even with his injury, Kendall Francois still belonged. Being on the football team gave him that. He was not some outsider. He was respected by the other kids. If anyone made fun of him, they didn't do it to his face. They'd have to be crazy to do that. He was bigger than almost all of them.

Appearance—with Francois it meant nothing. The fact was he didn't know what he was. Like most psychopaths, he was trying on identities to see what fit, what he could carry off.

He tried a new one on for his graduation photo. It is a stark reminder of how pictures can actually lie.

Francois strikes a studious pose, hands under his chin, posed in three-quarter style by the photographer. He wears an Afghan sweater, shirt and tie. His Afro hair is carefully cropped, but not too close to his skull. He has a high, brooding forehead. He wears great oversize glasses over languid dark eyes. He has a brush-cut mustache meant to make him look a little older, when it actually makes him look younger.

That year, every graduating Arlington senior was asked to put in their favorite quote. Under his name, Francois had chosen this quote from Hebrews 11:1:

> "Now faith is the substance of things hoped for, the evidence of things not seen."

Faith was something his victims' families would need to get them through the tragedies to come.

After graduating from Arlington, Francois enlisted in the United States Army. He did his basic training at Fort Sill in Oklahoma, and then was sent to an army base in Honolulu. When he got there, a serial killer was hard at work.

In the late 1980's, Honolulu, Hawaii, had several unsolved homicides of women who had died from strangulation. A serial killer was suspected. There was no clear suspect in sight.

While Francois was stationed there, more
women were murdered using the same modus
operandi (MO) or manner of murder. Ironically, the same problem existed back home.
There was a serial killer loose in the Mid Hudson Valley and the police seemed powerless to
catch him.

The first to be murdered was Juliana R.
Frank, twenty-nine, of Middletown, New York,
across the river in Orange County. She was
stabbed and killed on March 25, 1991. Her
body was later found on an abandoned railroad
bed in Middletown. Then came Larette Hug-
gins Reviere, thirty-four, also of Middletown.
She was killed on July 10. Her nude, stabbed
body was found in her house.

Christine M. Klebbe of the nearby town of
Goshen was next. She was reported missing on
July 1. Her body would later be found, stabbed
like the rest. Brenda L. Whiteside, twenty, of
Elmsford, was reported missing on July 20. A
short time later, her body was found in that
same town. She'd been stabbed. Angela Hopkins, Whiteside's cousin, was also reported missing on July 30 and her body was later found,
stabbed, in Goshen.

Finally there was Adriane M. Hunter of Middletown. She, too, had disappeared and then
her nude body was found. Another stabbing.

The case was finally broken when
Poughkeepsie police received an anonymous
phone call, a tip. Someone called to say that

Nathaniel White, thirty-two, of Middletown, should be looked at for the crimes. White had been paroled that April from state prison, where he'd served two years for robbing three convenience stores in Orange County. He was paroled in November 1989, rearrested on April 17, 1991, for kidnapping and assault. He plea bargained the charges down to unlawful imprisonment and was sentenced to nine months in state prison.

For violating his previous parole, three more months behind bars were tacked on to the sentence. Quoted in the *Albany Times Union* newspaper, Division of Parole Spokesman David Ernst said White showed no violent tendencies while serving his latest sentence.

Parole officials brought White in for questioning. Local and state police questioned him about the unsolved strangulation murders. In the opinion of law enforcement, he was not forthcoming in his responses to their questions. Put another way, he was lying. White eventually confessed, giving police the information that led to the recovery of the bodies of Klebbe, Whiteside and Hopkins. The others came later. White had killed all the women by repeatedly stabbing them. Some had also been raped.

Orange County District Attorney Frank D. Phillips was quoted as saying he didn't feel badly about White's recent parole. When someone asked him why, the DA responded with what could be any district attorney's epitaph:

"Because I'm only the district attorney; I'm not God."

On April 14, 1993, White was found guilty of six counts of second-degree murder and sentenced to a total of 150 years in prison. His legacy, if it could be called one, was a call to revise the state's missing person's procedures.

Three of the victims with similar descriptions were actually reported missing in July. But because two were from Dutchess County across the river and the other was from Orange County, police were not able to connect the cases for a week. There came a call for a sharing of information.

Police were reasonably certain that if this sharing of information policy were followed, there would be no more Nathaniel Whites slipping through their dragnet. But the police championing this methodology were the state police. The state police in New York are among the most highly trained and well-educated law enforcement professionals in the country. They are trained at a state-of-the-art law police academy in Albany.

In contrast, local police themselves have to pay for law enforcement training at a private police academy. Their hope is to catch on with a small-town force, like Poughkeepsie's, then go to a more urban area like New York or Hartford, to earn a better salary and more extensive benefits.

A cop got some experience in a small town setting, then took that and enlisted on the force of a larger town where his experience would get him some advancement. With Upstate New York unemployment higher than that in New York City, the small town could always find replacements.

Essentially, it was a pay as you go, learn as you go type of deal. Unfortunately, this arrangement played right into the hands of serial killers. They counted on police bureaucracy enabling them to continue in their killing careers.

When Kendall Francois was discharged from the service in 1994, he came back to Poughkeepsie and found a job as a substitute custodial worker for the Arlington School District. He worked in that position from May 1994 to April 1996. Then, he received a promotion.

From April 1996 to January 1997, he was a hall and detention monitor at his alma mater, the Arlington Middle School. His job was to make sure the kids were not unruly in the halls and the cafeteria. Because of his personal lack of hygiene, the kids began to call him "Stinky" behind his back.

Francois's tenure at Arlington Middle School was uneventful. But school official Ginny Jones would remember that many teachers complained that Francois behaved improperly with some girls, hugging them, playing with their hair, following them in the hall or making off-color jokes.

"I thought he was kind of inappropriate in his appearance, in his demeanor," said Jones.

Francois liked to wrestle with the kids.

"He would always want to wrestle and play

around," said Violet Reynolds, a student at Arlington during Francois's tenure there. "I never thought he was a threat."

She looked at Francois as a friendly face, someone dependable, and someone who could give her a ride home from high school wrestling matches when she needed a lift. Lori Johnson, a teaching assistant who worked with Francois at Arlington Middle School, remembered that he showed students wrestling holds he claimed to have learned in high school. Still, Francois was careful—there were no reports that he made inappropriate sexual contact with anyone there.

"He was a mild-mannered type of person. Quiet," recalled Donald Rothman, the school superintendent in an interview.

As much as Francois liked the work, the money wasn't very good, six dollars an hour or about forty-two dollars for a school day, but he lived at home and it was enough to cover his expenses. When he left in 1997, he went to work for the Andersen School. He only worked there for a short while before he was fired for some unknown reason.

Bill Siegrist's cops continued to work the street. The girls who had complained about Francois said he was big and dirty and liked to manhandle them. He was exceptionally strong and liked to show it. They said he liked it rough and he liked to dish it out, too. It was a lead worth further investigation.

Siegrist had his detectives maintain a periodic surveillance of the Francois home on Fulton Avenue. Nothing unusual happened. The cops then managed to get a street prostitute named Nancy Miles to allow them to wire her up to see if they could get Francois to, unknowingly, make some damaging admissions.

Miles was under orders that she was not, under any circumstances, to get into the car with the big man. When she did manage to talk with him on several occasions, standing outside while he sat behind the wheel, the microphone picked up nothing of value.

Stakeouts, surveillance, these activities cost police departments a lot of money, and police departments, like any public entity, have budgets. Unless they had something solid on Francois, the cops couldn't afford to follow him so closely. As for the missing women, it wasn't a priority. It couldn't be. There were no bodies, no crime scene. And while it would be nice to believe that every serial killer gets captured, that is just not the case.

According to Dr. Maurice Godwin, an investigative psychologist who works with police departments in developing "profiles" on serial killers, at any one time there are forty to fifty serial killers at large in the United States. Police don't like to talk about it lest the public panic, but it is a fact—not all serial killers are captured. Many continue to kill again and again.

In Washington State, the Green River Serial Killer was still at large after almost twenty years. He is believed to be responsible for the murder of forty-nine women, mostly drug-addicted prostitutes, between 1982 and 1984. The case was so cold only one detective was still on it full-time when DNA testing finally found a match in December 2001.

In Vancouver, British Columbia, twenty-one prostitutes were missing off the streets of the east side of the city. Like in Poughkeepsie, they had simply disappeared, leaving no crime scene. Which didn't mean they weren't dead. Of course, everyone really believed they were, but couldn't say it.

"We were agonizing what to do with the public," Siegrist recalls. "Do we go public and create a scare or keep going with the investigation without [letting the public know]? I have been a cop long enough to know you don't have all the answers."

There was no really good answer. If they went public, it would also be telling the killer they were now on his trail. That might cause him to go to ground and make getting him even tougher. On the other hand, maybe there was a way to turn such a public admission into an asset. Television's *America's Most Wanted* had shown how, done judiciously, the public's participation in apprehending a bad guy could be invaluable.

No one person, of course, could make that decision. Poughkeepsie is a small town after all and the decisions you make today will come back to haunt you tomorrow. *Everyone* is your neighbor. It isn't a good idea to anger them, especially the voters.

Anyone who lived in the town and city of Poughkeepsie got to vote for the Dutchess County Sheriff and District Attorney. City and town residents voted for their respective mayors. Catching a serial killer now, rather than later, would not only save lives, it might guarantee politicians' reelections.

In the end, the saner, practical heads won out. Siegrist and others involved in the case were allowed to speak on the record to the *Poughkeepsie Beat,* the weekly newspaper. The *Beat* was an upscale, local paper that featured hard news reporting in the front, and entertainment, lifestyle and sports articles farther back in its pages.

The article that appeared in April 1997 talked about the missing women and the possibility they had met their fate at the hands of a serial killer. What was curious was not the much-anticipated public reaction; the public didn't seem to care and no one panicked. What was more interesting was how the media reacted to the story.

The media reaction to the story was zero. No one seemed to care. The one daily paper in town, the *Poughkeepsie Journal,* didn't even pick up on the story. In a town with upscale pretensions, the murders of prostitutes hardly merited any ink. The media were not hounding the cops for a solution either, another break for Kendall Francois. Poughkeepsie's in-between geographic status had worked to the killer's advantage.

Poughkeepsie is too far from either New York

or Albany to be included in their daily TV coverage. Only a Poughkeepsie murder or murders covered on the Associated Press National Wire would break through onto the television news assignment editors' desks for further coverage.

The *Poughkeepsie Beat* got what amounted to an exclusive because no one cared to take it any further. As for the public reaction to the story, leads did come in to the cops. There were various kinds of weirdos, kinkos, deviants and other miscreants who were informed on by their neighbors. That made no difference either.

Throughout the first three-quarters of 1997, the investigation bogged down because of a lack of real suspects and real clues. For some reason, their killer had gone to ground. Maybe the *Beat* article had one reader who had taken it to heart. Maybe the killer had stopped because he was afraid of further news coverage.

Actually, nothing could be further from the truth. Kendall Francois had taken his respite from killing because he had a problem. A storage problem to be exact. By March 1997, Kendall Francois had a kill total of five women. Five corpses were rotting away in his attic. No one but Kendall knew they were there. His family would later claim they knew nothing about it, though Francois did become concerned that they might find out.

While the winter had slowed down the decomposition of the five bodies in the attic, they still smelled terribly. The odor of death permeated the house on Fulton Avenue. It leached out to every corner of the house.

"What is that smell?" McKinley Francois asked.

"Oh, that's just a family of dead raccoons in the attic," Francois replied.

He had gotten rid of them, he said, and was working on clearing out the smell. His mother, father and sister bought his explanation. Whether they really turned a "deaf" nose to the impossible smell is hard to say. If they did, they kept it to themselves. Apparently, they never complained again.

Until the odor diminished, Kendall Francois went about his business of picking up prostitutes, having sex with them, but not killing them. It was a personally turbulent time for Francois. It was in January 1997 that he had left his job at the Arlington Middle School and went to work at the Andersen School. Not long after, he was fired. He didn't give in to the murderous impulses raging inside him. He had to wait until the bodies didn't smell as much. Finally, in late October, the odor had begun to abate.

By then, the decomposition of the bodies was well along. Found at that stage, identification would have been difficult. But Gina Barone, Wendy Meyers, Cathy Marsh, Mary Healey Giaccone and Kathleen Hurley were a long way from being completely decomposed. They still had a lot of skin on their bodies. Kendall, though, didn't care about any of that. Who they were as people didn't matter.

He wasn't up nights having nightmares about them.

People who know their victims commit over seventy percent of murders. Out of the remaining thirty percent, serial murderers are a fraction of that percentage. Some serial murderers actually express remorse or regret for their actions.

The point is that purely evil men who kill with no heart or soul happens rarely. When it does, the killer is often possessed of an acute animal cunning that makes him able to escape detection until, and only until, luck plays a role in his capture.

Sociopaths like François who do not feel guilt exhibit a rare psychiatric disorder. Such individuals are not listed in the *DSM*. While sociopathy is acknowledged among psychiatrists as a legitimate mental condition, such individuals come under the "Antisocial Behavior" diagnosis in the *DSM*.

According to the *DSM*, the essential feature of Antisocial Personality Disorder is violating the rights of others. It is a condition that begins in childhood or early in adolescence and progresses into adulthood. The *DSM* does point out that this pattern of behavior is often referred to by other names, including "psychopathy" and "sociopathy." Deceit and manipulation are considered characteristics of this diagnosis.

People who exhibit this kind of behavior do not conform to social norms; far from it. They may exhibit unlawful behavior. Repeatedly, they may perform illegal acts, including property destruction. Harassment of individuals, robbery and illegal occupations are also characteristic. Frequently, they lie and cheat to get what they want, especially sex or power. They may act impulsively and fail to plan ahead.

Thus, when Francois killed the women in his house, he may have failed to plan in advance about what to do with the bodies. Seeing no other recourse except exposure, he secreted them in the attic, where they stank the place up.

People who exhibit this diagnosis may also have a high risk of unprotected sex with prostitutes. Francois was doing that, but so far he was lucky enough not to have contracted any debilitating diseases. Most important, sociopaths do not feel empathy. They are unfeeling, callous individuals who are contemptuous of the feelings and sufferings of others.

If ever a description was written that fit Kendall Francois, this was it. He could kill and would continue to kill without thinking twice about it. No thoughts of guilt, just survival. Kendall Francois cared nothing for his victims or the families they left behind. He cared nothing for the way they suffered and the lack of a decent burial. All Kendall Francois cared about was Kendall Francois.

The *DSM* further points out that Antisocial Personality Disorder tends to be exhibited in bleak, urban settings, where the individual exhibiting such a disorder is far down the economic ladder. Francois also seemed to fit these descriptions. Not only did he make little money at his jobs, he was picking on women in an urban setting. Yet it would have been literally impossible for any of Francois's teachers in his childhood and adolescence to diagnose him.

The *DSM* says that community samplings show that only three percent of men and one percent of women fall into this category. The diagnosis of Antisocial Personality Disorder itself cannot occur before the individual is eighteen years old. Thus, while Francois might have exhibited in childhood and adolescence certain signs of this disorder, like the fight he had in high school, the best anyone could have done was bring him to a psychiatrist for treatment. Even then, such treatment would probably have been ineffective. The *DSM* is clear that Antisocial Personality Disorder is a chronic illness, though its symptoms may lessen with age, particularly by age forty.

In 1997, Kendall Francois was only twenty-seven years old. His symptoms showed no signs of abating. He had displayed enough aggressive behavior with prostitutes to be one of the many suspects Siegrist had on his list. Yet nothing pointed to the big man directly. Without a "smoking gun," there was no point dragging him in for questioning.

September 1997

It didn't make the papers. It was just another prostitute missing and this one was black.

Newspapers and the rest of the media might say that everyone was given equal treatment— black, white, it didn't make any difference. Dead was dead, missing was missing and it was all fodder for the news machine. It was also a lot of garbage.

Newspapers give very little ink to missing women when they happen to be prostitutes. And black. Witness Michelle Eason. Eason was black, 5'2" and 115 pounds. Except for her skin color, she matched the general description of the other missing women. Eason had disappeared off Poughkeepsie's streets. No one could find her. Michelle Eason was subsequently reported missing on October 9. Like the others, her disappearance caused nary a ripple and failed to make the papers.

On the same day Eason disappeared, town police received a complaint that a 1984 two-door red Subaru was illegally parked at a medical office in the town. A quick computer search showed that the car was registered to Kendall L. Francois.

The Francois home was contacted and the family was asked to move the car. They did. Police later found it in a no-parking zone on Fulton Avenue. Tickets were issued on October 28, 29 and 30. The car was impounded on October 30 for failure to move it.

Police did not search it because there was no evidence the car had been used for anything other than simple transportation. Had they done so, they would probably have come up with microscopic traces of the people who had traveled in it, including loose hairs from the missing women. That would tie Francois forensically to the crime.

Francois was no dope. He wouldn't let that happen.

Police records show that Kendall L. Francois retrieved his car from the town of Poughkeepsie impound lot on October 31. He knew, then, that he needed to get rid of it, but he decided not to sell it.

Selling the car would be stupid. The cops could track it down to the new owner. Instead, he abandoned it where the police would never find it. He got rid of the plates, too. It was a disappearing act that a professional magician might envy. But he still needed transportation. Otherwise, he couldn't continue in his work.

As a human being, Francois was a slob. But as a killer, he was terribly neat and efficient in covering his tracks. He had become a real professional in his death work. If that was to continue, Francois needed a set of wheels, so he bought a new car, a late-model, white Toyota Camry. It was time to begin again.

November 1, 1997

It had been just over a year that the serial killer had been spreading his quiet terror through the Poughkeepsie community. People knew what was going on.

In the small coffee shop on Main Street called the Top Tomato, people sat at the counter and between gulps of bitter hot coffee, they discussed the missing women and what the hell the police were doing to bring the killer in. Talk turned to how the rival police departments from the town and the city were handling the investigation.

It was generally agreed that this rivalry was keeping them from pooling resources. While they twiddled their thumbs, women died. And why didn't the state come in? They had a killer on their hands who was killing with impunity.

No one was pacified by the elemental fact that the state had no jurisdiction to come into a murder investigation. The rationale was since the locals weren't doing anything, they should turn it over to the state, which could be done, and let them use their vast resources to solve the case.

"Pride goeth before the fall," and that was what was happening, residents believed. Neither the city nor town police departments would admit they were overwhelmed in the investigation. So the killings continued.

Bill Siegrist knew what people were thinking. He rode the streets of the city daily in his unmarked car. He stopped at Top Tomato on Main for coffee, at sandwich shops for submarine sandwiches. In over thirty years as a cop, he knew that was the best way to take the public pulse.

If the truth be known, Bill Siegrist was frustrated and feeling, not so much guilty that he couldn't do anything about the situation, but rather impatient. He wanted things to *move*.

What he got was another missing girl. Strangely
enough, this time the report came through the
police directly.

In October, Mary Healey Giaccone's mother
died. Mary's father, a retired New York State
corrections officer, personally came to the police to ask for help in locating his missing
daughter. He had reported her missing on November 13, 1997. Her parents had not spoken
with her in months. Siegrist soon discovered
that the girl had actually been missing since
February.

He checked around. No one had seen Giaccone. No one knew where she was. She had
vanished without a trace. Siegrist looked at the
description of the missing girl and saw that it
matched the rest. That made five. If Eason was
added to the mix, six.

Winter had come early to the Hudson Valley.
The temperature hovered in the low thirties.
And still the girls worked. Siegrist saw them on
his way home to Pleasant Valley. They were out
on Main Street plying their wares, selling their
bodies for the money to feed their addiction.
He shivered and it wasn't from the weather.

December 14, 1997

Finally, finally, the *Poughkeepsie Journal* published its first story about the missing women

under the headline IS THERE A SERIAL KILLER
LOOSE?

"She's my daughter . . . my baby. I don't
think she's ever coming back," Barone's
mother, Patricia, was quoted in the piece.

The article listed all the missing women:
Wendy Meyers, Catherine Marsh, Gina Barone,
Kathleen Hurley, Mary Healey Giaccone and
Michelle Eason. Also mentioned was the lack
of "public outcry" when prostitutes are murdered. The Nathaniel White case was cited to
prove the point.

"I fear the worst," Siegrist was quoted in the
article. "We have no bodies, no crime scenes,
but we have six missing women. I can't say we
have somebody out hunting women. I don't
know what happened."

That was true. Also quoted in the piece was
Gregg McCary, identified as "former director
of the FBI's elite behavioral sciences unit."

"This is, I mean, more than suspicious," said
McCary with classic understatement.

More understanding came from a "woman
on the street" comment.

"We are all human, and no one deserves to
get treated the way they're [prostitutes] treated,
the way they're spoken about. If that were my
child, I would love my child no matter what.
Because it's my child," said Julia Simpson, a
lifelong Poughkeepsie resident.

"Look what happened there," Simpson continued, referring to serial killer Nathaniel
White. "I can't believe these girls just disappeared; I'm sorry."

The case then went national. The Associated Press (AP) picked up the story and ran it on its national wire on November 21. The most intriguing paragraph of the story said, "Police are asking the FBI for help solving the cases of the women, who disappeared from the Poughkeepsie area from October 1996 to this month."

What the story was alluding to, which had not been made public, was that the Poughkeepsie Police Department had asked the FBI for a profile of the "bad guy." In turn, at a special December meeting with the FBI, Siegrist promised to keep them abreast of developments. But for the next month and a half, there were none.

In early January 1998, Bill Siegrist reported to work. The holidays were over and he had some paperwork to catch up on.

Sitting down at his desk, he began to look over reports that his detectives had filed. The detectives had narrowed down the list of possible killers. Besides Francois, there was another suspect. His name was Mark King, a sexual predator. He liked getting rough with prostitutes. They'd have to look a little harder at him.

Siegrist then came across a report filed by Detective Skip Mannain. In it, Mannain said that in the course of his routine interviewing of the area's prostitutes, Kendall Francois's name had come up yet again. The big man was up to his old tricks, Siegrist realized.

Francois had had sex with a girl where he

squeezed her throat just a little too hard. It had not only hurt; the girl had thought she was being killed. Then for some reason, he stopped, packed her up and brought her back to Main Street. Siegrist looked up, thought a minute, and then summoned Mannain into his office.

"Kendall Francois," said Siegrist. Siegrist then explained that he had read Mannain's report. "What's his pattern? During the day, I mean."

Mannain thought for a moment.

"He gets up, drops his mom off at work at the psych institute, where his mother works as a psych nurse."

Perfect. She'd had an in-house patient.

"What are you thinking, Lieutenant?"

PART TWO
The Cop

Six

Paulette Francois and her son Kendall exited their house through the side door into the alley. They tramped through the snow to the rear garage where Kendall opened the wooden door. Watching from across the street in a late-model, unmarked green Ford Taurus, Siegrist saw the big man hold open the car door for his mother.

Francois put his bulk behind the wheel of the midsize Toyota Camry. The car seemed barely able to contain him. He turned the key, the engine came to life and he immediately shifted gears and backed the car down the driveway. He executed a neat turn into the middle of the street, straightened his wheels, shifted again and gunned the motor. The car shot forward.

Siegrist made sure that Mannain, who was driving, stayed back at least one car length so the suspect would not get suspicious. They followed him to the Hudson Psychiatric Institute, watching as he pulled up the long, sloping driveway, and let his mother off at the top. Traveling back down, Siegrist and Mannain continued to follow as Francois made his left turn back toward town. They were just a few blocks away from the police station in one direction, and Main Street in the other. Knowing Francois's predilection for prostitutes, they knew he was headed for Main.

"Pull up behind him," Siegrist told Mannain.

A few minutes later, they were lounging at a light, ready for it to turn green. Slowly, methodically, Bill Siegrist uncorked his big frame from his car and walked up slowly to Francois's window. It was already rolled down. Siegrist leaned in. The first thing Francois eyed was the shiny lieutenant's badge in Siegrist's hand.

"Hi, Kendall. My name is Lieutenant Siegrist."

"Hello."

The cop ignored the greeting, but remained polite.

"Would you mind following me into headquarters? There's some questions I'd like to ask you."

"Not a problem, Lieutenant," Francois answered politely.

"Just follow me in," said Siegrist as he walked back to his car. He found it curious that Francois never once asked why.

For his part, Francois had to be wondering why he was being asked to come into the police station. What kinds of questions were the cops interested in asking? What answers were they looking for? Was he accused of having committed a crime?

Francois never let on what he was thinking. He just said nothing and allowed himself to be brought in. It was a curious reaction: meek, compliant, from a man suspected of serial murder.

Dutifully, Francois followed the unmarked car down Main Street, until they were finally at the police station. Siegrist pulled around back to the police lot on the south side of the building. He parked in one of the open spaces near what looked like a loading dock. Francois did the same.

Siegrist got out, and with Mannain on one side and him on the other, escorted Francois into the station. Since the man wasn't any more so a suspect in the disappearances than anyone else, he was not handcuffed. Since he had not yet been asked any questions about the women, he was not given his Miranda warning. That would come later; no sense in scaring the guy, but from the looks of how calm Francois was, it didn't look like much affected him. The guy acted like he had ice water in his veins.

Had Siegrist been more aware of the patterns of serial killers, he would have known that some act almost meekly at times. That is, until their killing instincts take over and they become insatiable in their desire to shed a victim's blood.

It had taken a while, over a year, but the cops finally had Kendall Francois in the conference room at police headquarters. Ordinarily, a suspect being interrogated was brought to one of the precinct's drab, gray interview rooms. Siegrist, though, had a specific reason for using the conference room.

"After you," said Siegrist, holding open the door for Francois, who walked in with a preternatural calm for somebody about to be interrogated about a series of disappearances. Nothing had been said about them yet. Francois looked around the room. He did not know it, but it had been specially decorated just for him.

Siegrist had gotten to headquarters early that morning and gone to work. He had pictures of the victims placed on one wall. On the other was a picture of Francois's Fulton Street house. A number of pictures, in fact, so Francois would know the cops had been shadowing him. As he stepped farther into the room and took a seat in a straight-backed chair that Siegrist offered, Francois's dark eyes picked out the photo of him from his high school yearbook. Then, he noticed the filing cabinets in the corner.

There was nothing special in those cabinets. But on the front of one drawer was a sign in block letters that said KENDALL FRANCOIS'S HIGH SCHOOL RECORDS. Another drawer was labeled KENDALL FRANCOIS'S COLLEGE RECORDS. The other two drawers in that four-drawer cabinet had labels in large block letters, too.

KENDALL FRANCOIS'S WORK RECORDS, said one.

KENDALL FRANCOIS'S BACKGROUND, said the other.

"We dummied it up," Siegrist would later recall. "There was nothing in them. And they were locked."

It was a giant bluff to get Francois to admit he was the Poughkeepsie serial killer. The cops figured they had a good fish on the line and hoped he would bite.

"We'll be back in a couple of minutes," said Siegrist, closing the door and leaving Francois alone in the room. He wanted him to stew awhile in his own juices.

Let the fat man think the cops had been concentrating on him and him alone. *Let him think they had him* and maybe, just maybe, he'd cave. Siegrist and Mannain retired to the lieutenant's office, where they killed a few minutes that they hoped would tick away like an eternity for Francois and make him crack. Finally, Siegrist wordlessly led the way back to the conference room and opened the door.

"Kendall," Siegrist began, as the two cops came in and took seats on either side of the big man, "we'd like to talk to you about the women that are missing."

"The missing women," Francois repeated, almost dumbly.

"We know you've had rough sex with a few of the girls on Main Street," said Mannain.

"I did?"

"We thought, well, maybe you had heard something," Siegrist continued.

"Like what?"

"Like who might have abducted these women."

Francois shook his head and said that he didn't know anything about that.

"We thought, since you hang out on Main Street, you might know the women."

"Like who?"

"Gina Barone. Wendy Meyers. Michelle Eason. Kathleen Hurley. Catherine Marsh. Mary Healey Giaccone."

Francois said none of the names rang any bells. He also did not admit to having sex with prostitutes.

"He admitted to nothing," Siegrist says. "He wouldn't go for anything."

Behind Francois's placid, emotionless facade, his mind was churning. He wasn't stupid; he was a college student. He knew the cops wouldn't have brought him in unless they really suspected him. But he also knew that they had nothing. Otherwise, they would have charged him. It gave Francois a feeling of power.

For his part, Siegrist knew he wasn't getting anywhere. If Francois was the guy, he was a stone-cold killer. Only one gambit was left.

"Kendall, we really appreciate you coming in today to answer our questions," said Siegrist. "But you know, cops, we like to dot the I's and cross the T's."

Francois just looked at him.

"What would really help us, and you, would be if you took a polygraph."

"You mean a lie detector test?"

Siegrist nodded. Francois didn't even think about it.

"Sure," he answered.

Siegrist found that to be an interesting reply. Either the guy really was innocent or he thought he could beat the machine.

Cops have implicit confidence in the machine's ability to root out the guilty and considered the machine's failure to be a rarity, something not even worth considering. Cops don't like to talk about the real truth: it isn't unprecedented for a guilty suspect to beat a lie detector.

Had they delved farther into the reasons why a guilty man could beat the machine, they would have had to acknowledge that it wasn't a foolproof method for discerning the truth. Not only would they lose confidence in the machine, criminals thinking they could get away with their crimes might think there was a way for them to control their physical responses. If they could do that, they could lie to a lie detector.

But such thoughts were just that—thoughts—nothing more, nothing less. Aberrations happened, but rarely. That's why they were aberrations; nothing to worry about.

Most small-town police departments like Poughkeepsie's do not have a separate unit devoted to polygraphing. It requires too much manpower and expertise, both of which would cost the taxpayers more money. In those circumstances, when a polygraph is needed, the city police apply to the state police for help.

The state police have barracks conveniently located throughout the state's counties. Some have polygraph units at their disposal. The nearest state police barracks with a polygraph, Troop K Barracks, is east of the city in the rural town of Millbrook. Siegrist quickly explained to Francois that they would transport him there.

It was a crucial moment. If Francois thought that there was any chance he would fail the test, he could say, "No." No one could compel him to take the test. Even if he were charged with six counts of murder one, with the death penalty staring him in the face, he didn't have to take the test. The Constitution gives the individual the right not to convict himself with his own admission of guilt. The smart suspect realizes that and agrees to nothing.

Francois said he had no problem going out to Troop K. His only condition was that they stop at his house on the way to pick up some things. Siegrist allowed him, escorted by Mannain, to make the stop.

Ordinarily, a cop can't just walk into a suspect's house unless he's there for an arrest. The suspect has to invite him in. Once inside, the cop is constitutionally free to roam anywhere he is allowed to. But if the suspect tells him to confine his movements to a specific space, the cop has no choice but to acquiesce. Otherwise, anything found as a result of such unauthorized probing is unusable in court because the suspect's rights were violated by an unlawful search. Only a court-ordered search of the premises could prevent this from happening. A court-ordered search would allow Mannain to look through Francois's home, but only for specific things enumerated in the warrant. Searches, to put it mildly, were a slippery constitutional slope that every good cop, and Mannain was one, is aware of.

"Skip, why don't you take Kendall out to his house and then over to Barracks K," Siegrist instructed him.

Skip Mannain nodded. He told Kendall Francois to follow him. They went through the station house. Francois noticed the close-packed desks, the way cops' eyes were averted as he went by. He didn't really care. He wasn't afraid. What was there to be afraid of? A machine?

Mannain took Francois out back and sat him down in the backseat of his unmarked police cruiser. He could also have put him in the front seat since he was not officially a suspect and hadn't been advised of his rights. Francois was going with him totally voluntarily. If he so much as indicated that he wanted the interview to cease and he wanted a lawyer, that would be the end of it.

Mannain knew he was on shaky ground. He had to give the guy a little leeway. He had to; otherwise, he'd clam up. A few minutes later, Mannain pulled the car in front of the house on Fulton Avenue. Francois led the way down the alley to the side door. As soon as he opened it, the stench hit Mannain like a knife in the gut. It was a combination of urine, feces, stale sweat and strange cooking odors. Lord, the place stunk to high heaven. And it was a mess.

There seemed to be garbage strewn everywhere. Mannain wanted to walk farther into the house, but Francois insisted, "Only up to my bedroom."

Mannain climbed the filth-encrusted stairwell. At the top, he followed Francois into his room. Francois made it clear again that Mannain was not to wander around.

"Skip Mannain is a clean freak," says Bill Siegrist. "He's a bachelor who lives by himself and he's always cleaning up after himself."

Indeed, Mannain presents an impeccable appearance. He's the kind of guy the marines love, a man who could pass a surprise inspection in his sleep. As he puttered around Francois's room, Mannain smelled feces and noticed soiled underwear with human waste lining the fabric. It was absolutely disgusting, even to a cop who, until then, thought he had seen, and smelled, it all.

Mannain was only in the home a few moments, before Francois said, "Let's go," and led the way down the stairs. Back outside, Mannain took in the cold January air in big, satisfying gulps.

He drove out Route 44, passing Pleasant Valley, where Bill Siegrist lived, until he got to the intersection with the Taconic State Parkway. A long scenic road, it went from Westchester County, which was a little north of New York City, and stretched more than one hundred miles north to the state capital of Albany.

Underneath the highway on the left was Troop K. Mannain took a left and pulled in.

They entered a low, not terribly modern-looking building with little or no character, which made sense considering it was just one of many barracks that housed the New York State Troopers. Mannain had called ahead and was led directly to a room where the polygraph had been set up.

The polygraph operator briefly explained to Kendall Francois how the machine worked. Mannain made sure to state once again that he wasn't a suspect and could leave at any time. But, by law, he had to give the warning everyone who has ever watched a cop show on TV is familiar with. While the results of a polygraph cannot be used in court, if Francois made any admissions of guilt, those could indeed be introduced as evidence. Thus Mannain administered the Miranda warning:

"You have the right to remain silent. Anything you say can and will be used against you in a court of law. You have the right to the presence of an attorney. If you cannot afford one, one will be appointed for you. Do you understand these rights?"

Francois said that he did. Then the wires were attached to Francois and the questioning began. The first series of questions were innocuous, things like, "Is your name Kendall L. Francois?" The idea was for the operator, and the machine, to become familiar with Francois's responses when he wasn't lying so that when he did, they would notice the sharp difference.

"All right, Mr. Francois, did you kill Wendy Meyers?" the operator asked.

"No," Francois replied.

"Are you responsible for Wendy Meyers's disappearance?"

"No."

"Did you kill Kathleen Hurley?"

"No."

"Are you responsible for Kathleen Hurley's disappearance?"

"No."

"Did you kill Catherine Marsh?"

"No."

"Are you responsible for her disappearance?"

"No."

"Did you kill Michelle Eason?"

"No."

"Are you responsible for her disappearance?"

"No."

"Did you kill Gina Barone?"

"No."

"Are you responsible for Gina's disappearance?"

"No."

"Did you kill Mary Healey Giaccone?"

"No."

"Are you responsible for Mary Healey Giaccone's disappearance?"

"No."

After the test, Francois was led to a conference room. He sat quietly, obediently, waiting for the results. In an adjacent room, Mannain

discussed the results of the test with the operator. It took a few minutes, but the verdict was
unavoidable.

Kendall Francois had passed with flying colors. According to the lie detector, the man
wasn't lying at all about the disappearances of
the women. He was not responsible. He was
telling the truth when he replied to the question, "Are you responsible for [their] disappearances?" Again, according to the machine,
he had been telling the truth. So why did Mannain still think he was lying?

Mannain thanked Francois for taking the
time to come in and drove him home. Less
than an hour after his lie detector test, Kendall
Francois was back, safely ensconced at home,
ready to kill again. Science be damned.

Seven

That night, Siegrist drove along Main Street on his way home. He saw Catina Newmaster working the street and pulled over to talk with her.

"Hi, Catina, how ya doing?"

"Okay, Bill."

Siegrist had known Catina Newmaster since she was a little girl. She had grown up in and around Poughkeepsie. The cop knew her to come from a family that had problems. How those problems had affected the girl, he didn't know. What he did know was that Catina had grown up to be "a likable person," far from the abrasive portrait the newspapers liked to paint of seasoned prostitutes, which Catina was.

"Listen, Catina, there's a guy out here and we don't know who he is. You need to watch out for him."

"I know," Catina said, nodding.

"Be careful who you're with," Siegrist cautioned.

"I will," said the girl.

Siegrist got back in his car and drove home, glad to be free, just for a while, away from the manhunt. And Catina? She went back to the street.

Siegrist was not one of those cops who believed in the lie detector's infallibility. Maybe the guy had lied and found a way to beat the machine. Maybe Francois's galvanic responses, his very nervous system, didn't respond like normal people's; that was why he could lie and get away with it. In the lieutenant's mind, Francois was still under a cloud of suspicion.

After Mannain briefed him on his trip to Kendall land, Siegrist had to wonder what kind of individual lived in such squalor, such human filth. And what about the man's family? How could they live like that, too? Siegrist was not willing to give up that easily. He wanted into the Francois home. They needed to get into that house.

Again.

Most serial killers keep some sort of memento of their victims. Even without the bodies, they could be used for conviction. And chances were, if he was the killer, those mementos were in the house. But how to get in?

Siegrist contacted the office of William Grady, the Dutchess County District Attorney. He was advised that the only way into the house was through a "fresh complainant"—someone who claimed anew that they had been assaulted by Francois. They would give them a reason to get a search warrant to get back into the house.

But who?

***

January 23, 1998

Her name was Lora Gallagher. Like Wendy Meyers, Gina Barone, Kathleen Hurley, Michelle Eason, Mary Healey Giaccone and Catherine Marsh, she was a prostitute who worked Poughkeepsie's streets. And, like the dead women, she knew Kendall Francois. Completing the similarities, Gallagher didn't like him either. The big man smelled and had rough hands.

Still, money was money, crack was crack and she just had to have it. Which was how she found herself getting into Francois's car, tooling along Main Street like they were casual shoppers, until the big man made a right turn, went down a few blocks, took a left and pulled into a driveway on Fulton Avenue.

He hustled her out of the car and up the back entrance to his bedroom. They negotiated a price, then began to go at it. In the middle of the "lovemaking," Francois really started getting rough. He began squeezing the woman's throat, harder and harder. He did it so tightly, her airflow was restricted and she was afraid she would pass out, or worse. Summoning every ounce of her strength, Gallagher wriggled free and pushed the big man off her. She demanded that he return her to Main Street immediately.

His heart beating wildly in his chest, Francois saw that for now his game was up. His blood lust needed to be satiated, but that could come later. Anytime he wanted. For now, if he continued with this girl, no telling what attention her struggles might bring him before she was dead. Francois needed to be in control and with Gallagher, he wasn't. Besides, she was in "that way," and that really turned him off.

A few minutes later, he dropped her back on Main Street. Shortly afterward, Gallagher shared her experience with one of her street friends, who in turn had a friend on the vice squad. The vice squad officer notified Siegrist of the incident. Mannain was sent out to question the woman. Gallagher told Mannain her story. Mannain convinced her to come in for further interviewing.

At the station, Mannain took a deposition from her about the incident. The deposition was a formal questioning under oath, taken down by a stenographer, admissible as evidence in court. With that done, all that was necessary was for Gallagher to sign it. The cops would then be able to arrest Francois and apply for a search warrant. They had their "in."

Siegrist had been keeping track of Gallagher's questioning. He had noticed how antsy she was. She just wanted to get out. He figured to keep her there just a little longer to get the deposition typed up and signed and then they'd be home free.

"I've got to go," Gallagher suddenly said. "I've got my period."

"She did not have on a pad and was bleeding through her pants. I could see it," Siegrist recalled. "I tried to convince her to stay a little longer."

But the woman would have none of it.

"I'm not a suspect. I know my rights," said the prostitute.

Gallagher had had enough experience with the law to know she was right. She walked out before signing the deposition. Now, they were as far away from cracking the case as they had ever been.

February 26, 1998

It would take another three weeks. At the end of that time, Siegrist convinced Gallagher to sign the deposition.

Because the alleged assault had taken place in Francois's home, which was just over the town line, he was brought into the Town of Poughkeepsie Police Headquarters and questioned there. He was brought in under a warrant for simple assault. Kendall L. Francois was duly advised of his constitutional rights. His fingerprints and mug shot were taken. Then, he did what some cops call "lawyering up."

He got an attorney to represent him. The attorney, of course, advised him to keep his mouth shut. Francois complied. He had taken enough government studies courses at Dutchess County Community College to know that was the smart thing to do.

Siegrist was frustrated. They had the guy under lock and key, for crissakes! But now he wouldn't talk to them anymore. Then things went from bad to worse.

The district attorney advised the lieutenant of detectives that the whole case was based upon the prostitute's word against Francois's. Francois had a cleaner record than she did. Not only that, the complainant Gallagher was not beating down the door to see the guy prosecuted. Clearly, she'd make a reluctant witness at trial. That was *not* how a conviction was won.

With the case against Francois shaky, Siegrist and company lost the opportunity for a search warrant. It was just a case of simple assault, the court reasoned. There was no reason to allow the cops to go rooting through the man's house. If they did that every time someone was charged with such a minor crime, they'd have cops beating down the doors of every minor felon in Dutchess County, not to mention having the case dismissed by the appeals courts for unreasonable search and seizure.

No, better to avoid that. Stay away from Francois's home, Siegrist was advised. And the cops couldn't talk to Francois either. Once a suspect requests a lawyer, all questioning ceases, unless the lawyer permits it, and Francois's wouldn't. Plus, Francois was granted bail while awaiting trial.

"We were told that every time we spoke with Francois, we had to tread lightly," Siegrist recalled.

Kendall Francois was a lot of things: killer, serial killer, liar, psychopath and psychotic. But one thing he wasn't was stupid. With so much scrutiny by law enforcement, he ceased his murderous activities. Right up until the time of his sentencing, Siegrist heard nothing that would enable him to pursue the big guy for the big crime.

May 18, 1998

Kendall Francois took his place at the side of his public defender in the Town of Poughkeepsie Court. Francois had claimed indigence since he wasn't gainfully employed and didn't have money to get his own lawyer. The fact that his parents owned a house worth six figures was irrelevant since it was in their names.

Siegrist was powerless to do anything but watch as the state supplied counsel to a suspected serial killer on an assault charge that the district attorney told him had been plea bargained down to a misdemeanor. Could anything be more ironic?

In the Poughkeepsie town court, unless the defendant requests it and is willing to pay for it out of his own pocket, there is no stenographer. The court's proceedings are "not for public view," according to the clerk for one of the court's judges. While every defendant is entitled to a public trial according to the Constitution, what isn't guaranteed is that someone will take the entire proceedings down verbatim. For that reason, there was no transcript of the disposition of the charge against Kendall Francois. All that exists is a computer record of the result.

On May 18, 1998, Kendall Francois pleaded guilty to a charge of assault in the third degree, a misdemeanor, and was sentenced to fifteen days in the county jail. With time off for good behavior and credit for the time he was in actual custody, Francois served just seven days. He was back in action on May 25.

As he walked out of county jail, Kendall Francois realized what a good day it was. It was sunny and nice. The free air felt good. There were no more charges pending against him. He had served his time. The relentless police scrutiny of his activities that he had had to endure in the preceding months had been curbed. The odor in the attic was abating.

It was time to kill again.

Getting to Dover Plains was not easy. Situated in the eastern section of Dutchess County, the only way to get there from Poughkeepsie was to take Route 55 east out of town. There was no other road that would go that far east.

Ten miles outside of Poughkeepsie, the surroundings changed from suburban to rural. Farms dotted the landscape. Apple orchards crowded together, ripe for the fall harvest. Just before Tymore Park, Route 55 came to a crossroads. The fork on the left was East Noxon, a county road made out of old tar and cement dust.

Taking a left onto it, East Noxon ambled for a few miles until it became Burugzal Road. Changing its name as it wound east through isolated towns with populations that barely reached a thousand, the road, actually listed as County Road 20 on the map, finally met up with State Route 6, less than ten miles from the Connecticut border. The area was so rural that a few miles north, the Appalachian Trail cut through the countryside.

Going north on 22, the town of Dover came up in the distance. Before getting there, you passed the Valley Psychiatric Center. Then just a few more miles north, the road finally came into the town of Dover Plains. It was the kind of place people leave from, not go to.

There was really no hope in Dover Plains. When Sandra French grew up there in the 1950's, there was no industry, just a few stores, a library, a city hall and that was about it. By the 1960's, when she was in high school, things were still the same. That was the trouble with Dover Plains—things were always the same there. Time stood still. Things never changed. That included the kids.

Sandra Jean French's 1965 senior high school yearbook photo shows a mature young woman who looks ready to take on the world. The black-and-white picture shows a dark-haired girl with striking dark eyes, a nice nose and full lips, wearing a chic, black-knit turtleneck.

"Sandi," as her friends knew her, had been a popular girl in Dover Plains High School. In her yearbook, she gave her likes as "1957 Chevys, horses, parties" and dislikes as "snotty people, Monday morning, and hangovers." Her future plans included attending air stewardess school and marriage. She'd enjoyed many of the school activities and was proud to have chorus; library council; intramurals; future nurses' club; and pep club as accomplishments.

All in all, French sounded like any young girl of her time. Active in school activities, like many women who were brought up in the 1950's, she had decided to follow the traditional role of wife and mother. But Sandi was different: before she did any of that, she yearned to try out the glamorous life of an airline stewardess.

As a stewardess, she would get to travel all over the world. For free. She would meet all kinds of interesting people. Maybe, just maybe, one of those interesting people would be her Prince Charming. It was a grand fantasy, for that's what it was, fantasy pure and simple. The most insightful entry in her yearbook listing was not her future ambitions, but rather the way she dealt with her present. Didn't anyone at the time think to wonder why a young girl of nineteen's "dislikes" included "hangovers"?

At the time, the legal drinking age in New York was twenty-one. Most kids, who lived in upstate New York, as Sandra French did, violated that because of curiosity about alcohol. And it was hard not to be curious. Alcohol, and its abuse, was a distinct part of the area's culture. If you didn't drink, you weren't a regular type of person. For the women, trapped by babies and husbands in low-paying jobs, drinking was an easy escape.

Yet how many young girls like Sandra French had become so familiar with alcohol and its effects that by the age of nineteen, they abhorred hangovers? It did not augur well for French's future that she was so familiar with the effects of liquor. The mention of alcohol and its effects in her yearbook listing was a clear tip-off to Sandra French's future substance-abuse problems. Unfortunately, nobody saw that. Even if they had, what could they have done, except counsel her to drink in moderation?

Horse farms dotted the landscape of Dutchess County and after graduation, French, an avowed horse lover, became a horse attendant on some of them. Mucking out stables was not an alien thing to her. Neither was being stoned.

From alcohol, she turned to harder drugs, eventually becoming an addict, turning to the streets to support her habit. She would spend much of the next thirty years going in and out of jail for drug and prostitution arrests. In between, she found time to have three kids, one of whom was Heidi Cramer, who in 1998 was twenty-nine years old. Cramer recalled that her mom never tried to hide her drug addiction and prostitution.

"That's what made her [who she was]," Cramer would later tell a local paper.

They lived, not in Dover Plains, but in the nearby community of Oniontown, which Cramer described as a rural New York version of the Ozarks, "almost like a hillbilly community."

But what made French's life a little bit more out of the ordinary than her lifestyle and arrests was an incident that occurred when her daughter, Heidi, was twelve years old.

In 1981, Sandi French shot a man. The man lived but, ironically, it was Heidi who was branded. For the next few years in her neighborhood, Heidi became known as the "daughter of the shooter." It wasn't a pleasant feeling.

Sandra Jean French had not become a nurse, or a stewardess, or any other kind of professional. She had become a jailbird, a drug-addicted prostitute. Life had not happened the way it was supposed to all those years before in Dover Plains High School.

On June 11, 1998, French returned one more time to Dover Plains to visit friends. Afterward, she said good-bye and drove away. Four days later, on June 15, police found her car abandoned in the Arlington area of Poughkeepsie, within a few blocks of the Arlington Middle School where Kendall Francois used to work.

Heidi Cramer reported her mother missing. The detectives looked into it. Siegrist and his men were stymied. They could find no trace of French. The lieutenant suspected that their serial killer was at work again.

June 12, 1998

Prostitutes have lives off the street, too. Take Sandi French.

Cramer was expecting and French was about to become a grandmother. French was just as excited as her daughter Heidi Cramer was. French called her daughter at least three times a day to make sure she was okay and brought meals over. Sometimes, French shopped the Poughkeepsie mall, buying clothes for the baby about to make its way into the world. All in all, it was one of the most exciting and fulfilling times in French's life. But, she still had to make a living to support her habit.

The day French met Francois again, it had been a hot morning. Her feet felt hot through her shoes as she walked the steaming pavement of Main Street looking for a john. That was when the fat man came along.

It was hard not to think of Kendall Francois in any other way. He didn't give off the air of solidity that some big men did; he seemed like a big, round, soft, black version of the Pillsbury Doughboy. Sandi knew Kendall from other liaisons.

Francois picked her up in his white Camry. They quickly negotiated the price for sex and then he drove back to his house. As he got out of the car, he looked around for a moment. No one was there. No one was watching. If they were, they were behind curtains and did not make their presence known. And if they were watching and knew something, they must have been afraid, because they never said anything.

French marched to her doom up the rear stairs of the Francois home. Though, of course, she didn't know that. She had had sex with

Francois before so the absolute filth of his home would have come as no surprise, nor the odors of shit, stale sweat, old urine, rancid grease and something else French wasn't able to place. You really needed a gas mask to breathe easily in the place.

Francois himself was no better. When French had sex with him a few minutes later, she would have realized he stank worse than a dead skunk in the road. But Sandra French was beyond expectation or disappointment.

Heidi Cramer had thought that her mother was honest when she talked about her arrests for drug addiction and prostitution. She wasn't, because Sandra French couldn't admit to herself that she had screwed up her life. She could not deal with how her drug addiction had cost her precious years with her children, how her self-destructive life led her to commit violence. French only took responsibility for the moment and that was mostly to feed her addiction. To do so meant prostituting herself. Which was how she happened to be with this smelly john. Betraying the quick hands that had helped him turn the tables on unwitting wrestling opponents in high school, Francois's fingers grabbed French's throat like a vise. Startled, she grabbed for them and struggled to remove them.

She struggled all right, all 5'0" and 120 pounds of her against the bulky 6'4" ex-wrestler. Francois squeezed harder. He was determined to choke the life out of her. Francois twisted around and brought her body down to the bed, still holding hard to her throat. The woman was beginning to struggle less now, her eyes bulging out, her tongue flopping outside her mouth. The next moment, when her hyoid, or throat bone, cracked, all that Sandra French was and all she would ever be was eliminated as she descended into death. For Francois, though, death was not the end.

He took the body into the bathroom. He gently placed French's corpse in the tub, turned on the water and bathed her. When he was satisfied that she was clean enough, he took the body out, and dried it with a towel. He had to do that; otherwise, there'd be a trail of water to the woman's final resting place. No way did he want to be discovered.

Francois picked up the body and slung it over his shoulder. Hands free, he ascended to the attic and dumped it with the other bodies. He could see that things were beginning to get a little crowded. The next day, when no one was around, he went back up to the attic and got French's body. Then he went down to the first floor, and down farther to the basement. The basement was as much of a dark mess as the upstairs. It looked like the burial ground of lost and broken household objects.

The crawl space was in the rear of the basement, sort of a shelf that ran right under the house. He propped the body up against the top of it, raised himself up and, making sure he didn't knock his head against the low ceiling, climbed into the crawl space. It was a field of dirt that stretched the length of the house.

Then he reached back and pulled French up. It was easy for the big man; she hardly weighed anything at all.

Stooping low, he placed the body about five feet back from the lip of the crawl space. He dug a shallow pit and then pushed French's body into it. He began piling dirt on top of her until most of French's body was covered. Afterward, looking down at the shallow grave, he had to smile. It was a good job. Nice. Neat. Satisfying. And the best part was, it wasn't over, not by a long shot.

A few days later, Heidi Cramer gave birth to a healthy child. Had she lived, it would have been Sandra French's first grandchild.

Eight

Siegrist was anxious. He wanted to get the son of a bitch already. It was a man, no doubt, because no one knew of a case where a woman went around disposing of prostitutes, unless it was some cheesy TV movie that bore no relationship to reality. Sitting beside the Hudson River again, eating a sandwich and gazing out at the waterway named after the famous Dutch explorer, Siegrist thought about the case and the suspects.

"From past experience, I reminded myself to be open-minded. Many times, you fail to solve a crime because you don't have the right pool of suspects at the beginning and you don't trust your own instincts."

Bill Siegrist's instincts had caused him to zero in on two men.

"I felt Kendall Francois was a [strong] suspect."

But there was another who also fit the profile of the man they decided they were looking for. He was Mark King and his name had come up in a computer search of sexual felons. Same as Francois, he was in his twenties and had a history of getting rough with prostitutes.

King had to be looked at seriously. He lived in a remote, terribly rural area of the county. He could dispose of a hundred bodies if he wanted and no one would be the wiser. Again, there was no direct evidence to indict, but the county was willing to spend the funds to search the area surrounding King's land. To do the job, Siegrist called in the Ramapo Search and Rescue Dogs.

The scent of death tends to be a morbid subject. Most people don't like to consider that the smell of a body is so distinctive that someone, human or animal, can be trained to smell it.

While humans might have some experience in discerning the smell on the basis of past experience, it was Bill and Jean Syrotuck who refined the concept of the air-scenting search dog and adapted it to wilderness situations. In 1972, they formed the American Rescue Dogs Association (ARDA).

Since that time, the Syrotucks' organization, ARDA, had established certified chapters around the country. These chapters were actually composed of dog trainers and their charges; the latter were trained in all kinds of search and rescue situations. They could smell people alive or dead in avalanches, earthquake-ravaged buildings, water and, of course, out in the wilderness or woods.

ARDA innovations included the development of standards and training for air-scenting dogs. This included the first work done on scent behavior under different terrain and weather conditions and the development of a national evaluation system for ARDA units, wherein each ARDA unit must periodically pass a rigorous field examination by ARDA evaluators. In addition, Bill and Jean Syrotuck developed the sector search method, using multiple dog/handler teams simultaneously, and they compiled the first study of victim behavior, now used in search management courses nationwide.

One of the many honors the organization would gather was in 1977, when the Ramapo Search and Rescue Dogs Unit, based in Chester, New York, became the first of its kind to be used in a major disaster, the Johnstown floods. Since that time, the Ramapo squad had gone on to greater fame in similar rescue situations.

Siegrist knew that a search of the area around King's cabin required these specially trained dogs, which some in law enforcement sometimes called "cadaver dogs." That was why he called the Ramapo Search and Rescue Dogs for assistance. Headed up by Tim and Penny Sullivan, the Ramapo group promised to help.

"It was a Saturday, in June 1998, when the Ramapo dogs came up," Siegrist recalled. "They are all volunteers."

Which was why he couldn't say much when some of the dog handlers and their charges came a bit late. It was understandable, though. The search was in a remote section of the county and just getting there was difficult. Once there, the party went to work. The dogs were loosed over a twenty-mile-square area. Besides densely wooded brush, they would have

to scent along a nearby railroad track. There
are many instances in the annals of criminal
justice where killers dumped their bodies near
railroad tracks; every inch of ground needed
to be covered.

The dogs sniffed and howled their way
through the cool June day. They followed trail
after trail, dug their noses into brush and bark,
around pines and oaks, evergreens and poplars.
Leaves fallen from autumns past had dried out
over time and crunched under the dogs' paws,
toughened by outdoor work to the consistency
of sandpaper. Siegrist watched them do their
work, amazed at how well the dogs handled,
hopeful they'd turn up something.

They didn't. As afternoon wore into evening,
Siegrist could see that the search was hopeless.
If King was their man, he had hidden the bodies pretty well. Siegrist's thoughts drifted back
to Kendall Francois.

Maybe I should bring the dogs over to his house,
Siegrist thought.

While the law would not allow a search of
the Francois home without due cause, there
was nothing to stop Siegrist from having a
Ramapo dog sniff around the Francois home.
As long as he stayed on town property—the
house's frontage—he was legally okay. Probably.

Probably. He wasn't a lawyer, but he'd had
enough experience going in and out of court
over the years for hearings on suspects he had
arrested that he knew something about the
Fourth Amendment's guarantee against unrea-

sonable search and seizure and what the courts forbade a cop to do without proper cause.

Should he bring them over to Francois's home and have them sniff around outside? If he did, would their keen noses pick up the unique odor of death?

In the end, he decided against it.

"I hadn't wanted to ask too much of the volunteers," Siegrist says. "They are, after all, volunteers."

After the dogs left, Siegrist drove home to Pleasant Valley through the cool night air. Though it was hard to believe, frost was still possible in June in the Hudson Valley. Under tree-shrouded canopies, Siegrist drove into and out of little pools of light cast by a combination of sources—the full moon, the few passing headlights, a street lamp—as he passed through small towns.

"Could we have saved some lives if we did?" Siegrist would later ask himself. "If I had told them to search, would the dogs hit on it [the smell of the corpses] and what would it have meant to the case? Could we have saved more lives?"

Those questions would haunt Siegrist for years to come.

Lucy Degaudio, short, petite and twenty-nine, had known Kendall Francois for a while. She did him favors.

Kendall, as she referred to him, would give her rides when she needed them. That, of course, was a prelude to their business transactions: Degaudio pimped for him.

Francois would pull to the curb where Degaudio was standing on Main Street. He'd get out and come up to her, his heavy feet crunching on the glass that littered the street. The glass was from empty crack vials and soda bottles. Francois would offer Degaudio money for women. If she wanted the money, which she did, she would get some of her "associates" to perform sex acts for the stinking, fat man.

There wasn't anything unusual about the practice; other guys did it. But Francois was known to be a bit rough with the women. Yet they came back for more. They continued to go with him to the house on Fulton Avenue, to inhale the stink because they needed the money to feed their drug habits.

Sometimes, when Kendall was in the mood, he wanted Degaudio. On those occasions, she would be chauffeured by the man to his house, taken up to the second-floor bedroom and would have sex with him. It was pretty disgusting, what with the guy's girth—he was so heavy he had "bitch tits." Coupled with the odor, it was truly disgusting, but, hey, a buck's a buck.

Sometimes when Lucy was with the man that she called Kendall, she would be fucking him and her mind would drift off to her niece Robin, whom she loved to play with. Then, after he had come and pushed her around a bit, he would take her back to Main Street and drop her off, just like the rest of the Main Street women who went with him.

* * *

August 5, 1998

It was a hot day in the Hudson Valley, perfect for dipping in the river, a backyard pool, a lake, whatever was wet and handy. For the women on Main Street, though, it was business as usual.

Lucy Degaudio was streetwalking, looking to pick up a john when she saw the white Toyota pull over to the curb. Kendall was inside. She couldn't believe that for such a big, imposing guy, he had such a sweet-looking face.

"Oh, hi, Kendall," said Degaudio, sticking her head through the open passenger-side window and flashing her almost perfect, white teeth.

Her teeth were a great asset. Most of the girls in her profession had not taken care of theirs. They were cracked, discolored and, in some cases, black. But hers were pearly white and she could use them.

"Hi, Lucy," he answered in a flat tone. "Get in."

Degaudio got in.

"We'll go back to my house," he said simply.

It was clear—if she wanted to get his money, she had to go back with him. That wasn't the best scenario. It would take time. Easier to do it around the corner in a deserted lot.

Whatever. It was hot. Best to get a move on so she could finish up and get back out there. Time was money in her profession.

Francois drove slowly over to the house, making sure to obey all speed limits and traffic rules. He wasn't going to get caught like that idiot on Long Island, the serial killer Joel Rifkin, who was finally captured after he was stopped for a moving violation.

No, sir! Kendall Francois was a lot smarter than that.

At the house, Francois pulled up the driveway between the house and stopped the car. He got out, opened the garage door, got back inside and drove the car into the space. In the garage, next to the car, was a soiled mattress. The windows were open and Lucy could smell new construction, that unique, sweetish odor of pine boards and concrete. The garage had a recently poured concrete floor.

"Let's have some privacy," said Francois, lowering the garage door.

For some reason, Degaudio was apprehensive.

"Why don't you leave it open a crack, why don'tcha?"

"What do you think, I'm going to hurt you?"

She hoped not. Degaudio had a daughter and she was hoping to get the money for her birthday present by having sex with Francois. They agreed on a price of twenty dollars. They got down on all fours on the mattress like rutting dogs. Quickly, Francois mounted her. She turned onto her back.

It felt like a heavy stone had been laid across her chest; she could hardly breathe. The guy looked like he weighed over 300 pounds. If he wasn't the biggest trick she had ever had, he was probably close to it. Looking up, she saw Francois's contorted face as he pumped. The sweat poured down his face as he pushed, the liquid dripping onto her. She became aware of something else—her vagina was hurting.

The guy was just too damn big. He wasn't just filling her up; he was stretching her. Her vagina hurt. To Degaudio, it seemed like the session went on for an eternity. It was actually only about twenty-five minutes, when she asked him to stop.

"Kendall, just please get off me."

"Shut up! Shut up! My sister's asleep," he hissed.

Degaudio began to cry. Something was really wrong. She wanted out. Fast. And she didn't care who heard. She screamed for him to get off her. His eyes were bulging, his breath coming in short, hard gasps.

"You fucking whore! You bitch! You cocksucker!" he screamed at her.

Why had he gotten so angry? Maybe he thought she was pushing him and he didn't like that. Degaudio was, since prostitutes are on the clock. They got paid for their time. And this guy just wasn't doing his business.

Francois's anger and rage boiled up. She never saw it coming.

The punch caught her flush on the chin. Just like a boxer in the ring, her brain responded to the brute force of the blow by hitting against the side of her skull on the inside. It seemed as though she were falling into a black hole. Then, there was nothing and she blacked out.

There was no telling how long she was unconscious, but when she came to, Francois was looming above her, a tall, towering, menacing creature with a meaty paw going for her throat. Degaudio reached out with her hands and they sank into the Pillsbury Doughboy fat that covered his body. Degaudio got a good grip and, with a mighty heave born from desperation that she could never again muster in a million years, she pushed him off her.

Kendall came right back for more.

"Help, help!" she screamed. "Someone help me!"

"You stupid, little, fucking whore! Keep your big mouth shut, you cunt!"

"Help, help, get me out of here!"

Degaudio was still pushing at him, struggling, when suddenly, the big man went limp. Francois had quickly figured out that this one was not going easily and that if he continued, her screaming would attract the kind of attention he could not afford, not if he expected to remain free to continue. He had already had one run-in with the law this year. He was not about to make it two.

Francois took a few steps and jerked the garage door open. Sunlight flooded the confined space. To Degaudio, it was literally a ray of hope. If she survived, she knew she was being redeemed from the brink. Then, she did a stupid thing.

She told Francois she needed a lift back.

The man had just tried to kill her and she was hustling a lift from him because she didn't want to walk home. He could still hurt her, even in the car. But she was exhausted and didn't feel like walking. She didn't figure he'd hurt her in broad daylight.

The car door was opened and she got in. Francois slammed it behind her so hard, it felt like it could come right off its hinges. Francois got in behind the wheel, slammed his door just as hard and then pulled out. He stopped long enough to close the garage door, got back in, backed out and headed down toward Vassar.

At the corner, he took the left and headed back to Main Street. She wanted to go to her apartment, which Francois had been to before for "business" purposes. Instead, Francois decided to drop her down on Main Street where he'd found her. He figured the bitch could find her own way home. And that was what he did. Wordlessly, she got out and walked home.

About six hours later, she got a call at home.

"This is Kendall," he said.

"Yes?" she replied apprehensively.

"If you don't keep your mouth shut, you're going to be the victim of a crime," he told her.

The next day, which was Monday, Francois called again.

"I'm busy, Kendall."

Not more than fifteen minutes later, Francois was outside her window. Degaudio's second-floor apartment was in an old building on Main Street.

"Lucy, Lucy," he called up.

Degaudio went to her window. She was surprised, and not a little apprehensive, when she saw Francois on the sidewalk calling up to her.

"Come on down and go shopping with me," Francois called, trying hard to be polite and easygoing. "I need a woman's touch," he continued, smiling. "It's for my mom. I want to get her an antique table."

Degaudio didn't have to think twice.

"I'm busy, Kendall. I told you that on the phone," she shouted down.

She noticed his eyes. They were faraway, distant, as though he were a different person. He seemed unsure of himself, wanting to do something, but not sure how to go about it. He tried pleading again, but to no avail.

Degaudio had felt sore ever since she had gotten home the day before. Her chin where he'd punched her ached. Her vagina felt like someone had tried to tear it up.

Francois knew that his powers of persuasion were not enough to overcome the woman's resistance. He got back into his car and drove away. Degaudio closed the window and retreated into her apartment. Soon after, Lucy Degaudio went back to her life on the street, smoking crack when she got depressed to take the edge off. She went back to anonymous men with money who paid for her crack, which she bought from her dealers.

Degaudio would later wonder why she had not let the police know of her encounter with Francois. Maybe she thought she wouldn't be believed. Maybe she didn't want to be known as a "rat," though why anyone would want to protect Francois was unfathomable, unless she thought that by coming forward, she would be arrested for prostitution. Common sense would have told her that the police didn't care about her; it was the man responsible for the missing women that they wanted.

Ultimately, she didn't come forward because it had been so traumatic. The man had come this close to killing her. She could just as easily have awakened in heaven or someplace else, instead of this world after Francois had knocked her out. She had almost died.

For weeks after their encounter, Degaudio had nightmares about Francois. In them, he came back to finish the job. Who knew what would happen if she spoke out against him?

Suppose the cops couldn't make a case against him for assaulting her? He could come after her. Who would protect her? She was a prostitute, after all. Who cared about her? Certainly not the public, who treated her like dirt. The cops? They tolerated her only because they had to. They would just as soon sweep her off the street like some common criminal.

So Lucy Degaudio said nothing. Later, much later, she, like Siegrist, would wonder about what might have been and the lives she might have saved.

Nine

August 12, 1998

Senior Investigator Jimmy Ayling remembers the day well.

"I was asked to go down to Poughkeepsie and aid in the formation of a combined task force to catch the Poughkeepsie serial killer," he recalls.

In Ayling's job, helping to run the state's ViCAP program, such cooperation was not out of the ordinary. That was the idea of ViCAP—to put one segment of law enforcement in touch with another toward the same goal of catching the "bad guy."

One of the primary things Ayling was prepared to offer as his end of the deal was access to ViCAP's powerful computer databases, including their Abduction/Molestation File. The latter could be programmed to correlate case-specific data relating to stranger abductions. Perhaps more important to the case at hand, ViCAP could provide time lines for potential or suspected serial predators.

This was cutting-edge police technology that made a cop's job easier and the public safer.

What was unusual about the task force Ayling had been asked to join was it was being kept a secret from the public.

Ayling got on the New York State Thruway at Exit 23. He took his ticket from the tollbooth attendant, placed it on the seat beside him and headed to the left, down the ramp that said NEW YORK CITY—SOUTH. It took an hour and fifteen minutes before he got to Exit 18 in New Paltz. He got off, paid the toll and took a hard right, passing a diner. About two miles down, the road dead-ended and he took a right onto Route 9W. He passed a sign that said HIGHLAND. He remembered it as the place Wendy Meyers had come from.

A little farther on, he took the right exit, which twisted around, and he came to another tollbooth. *Lord,* he thought, *we sure pay a lot of tolls in this state.* This time it was only a dollar and then he drove out onto the Mid Hudson Bridge. On the other side, in Poughkeepsie, he drove down Church Street, took a left and went to the district attorney's office. He parked across the street, went into the building on time and was shown to the prearranged room.

Already there were Bill Siegrist and Skip Mannain from the city police and Detectives Bob McCready and Arthur Boyko from the town police. Ayling represented the state police. The idea of the task force was to pool all the resources from these various branches of local and state law enforcement toward the common goal of bringing the killer to ground. At the meeting, arrangements were made to formalize sharing of information and how the group would work together.

The final member of what would be the combined task force, whose sole job was to track down the serial killer preying on the area's prostitutes, was Dutchess County District Attorney William Grady. It was Grady who had decided not to make the task force's existence public for a week, giving them time to set their communications systems up and also to let the killer think he could still take advantage of the seeming disorganization that had existed before.

Let the killer be a little overconfident; maybe he would do something in the next week to trip himself up and then they would be right there to catch him!

Siegrist drove home that night, confident that things were moving forward. When he saw Catina Newmaster again, working Main Street, he stopped and got out of the car. Newmaster was a slight blonde in her late twenties. She looked like a fondly remembered girlfriend, not some drug addict feeding her addiction through prostituting herself. She looked as though the debasement had not gotten to her, at least not yet. One more warning couldn't hurt.

"Catina, are you being careful?" Siegrist asked.

"Sure am, Bill," she said, nodding.

And she had been. Still, as Siegrist drove home, he felt apprehensive. Not just about Catina, but the whole operation. Law enforcement had cut across normal bureaucratic lines to agree to cooperate fully for the greater good. It was a formal agreement to develop and share information. And that was good.

Maybe someone would develop a lead, or examine an old one that would lead to the guy. More likely, though, the break would come through dogged, deliberate police work, the kind that doesn't make headlines. It could be like the "Son of Sam" case in the 1970's.

Serial killer David Berkowitz had terrorized New York City, killing people throughout the boroughs, until he was traced through a random parking ticket, which led to his capture. Or maybe it would be something as simple as stopping the bad guy for a moving violation and finding bodies in his truck. That was how police on Long Island had captured serial killer Joel Rifkin in the 1980's.

Maybe they wouldn't capture the guy at all. At that time, Washington State's Green River Killer was still at large. So was the Vancouver Serial Killer, who, like Poughkeepsie's, preyed on prostitutes. Siegrist knew that no matter how many men they put in the field, the guy was going to continue to kill until they stopped him.

How long that would take, he wasn't prepared to say.

The state had now deployed its officers and its full technological resources behind capturing the man behind the disappearance of the six Poughkeepsie women. The city and town of Poughkeepsie were also part of the task force. While the surrounding rural police departments were not, at least formally, they, too, would be contributing information that seemed relevant. All of this, the time and the money, was dedicated to tracking down one unknown man.

The FBI profile supplied to Siegrist of the man they were tracking was the same generic profile the bureau supplied in any case involving a serial killer. The killer was white, late twenties to thirties, had difficulty with romantic attachments, couldn't hold a job, was from the middle to lower-middle class and had probably tortured animals in his youth. In other words, it was of absolutely no value.

Not only did much of that profile fit half of the single men in America, 99.9 percent of whom were not serial killers, it did not apply to African Americans. It was reverse racism: the bureau theorized that few black serial killers existed and the model was adjusted accordingly. It was no secret within law enforcement that FBI profiles were invariably the same. Cops knew they were of no practical value. It was just on the off chance the FBI might get something right that they were contacted.

Regardless of the paperwork they supplied, the bureau did not speculate on where any individual killer might be found. And without that information, it was back to the proverbial "needle in a haystack" scenario.

At the very moment the task force was scrambling to find him, the man they were desperately seeking, Kendall Francois, continued to cultivate an unassuming, middle-class exterior while continuing to live his real life in the shadows.

What was reality to him, what gave him pleasure, was flushing out the city's prostitutes for his next victim. Like Jack the Ripper a century before him, he had not only a taste for the street women and a desire to possess them, he had an overwhelming passion to extinguish their lives. Francois didn't know it, but if he killed two more, he would surpass the Ripper's total.

But unknown to the hunter, others were attempting to put him in *their* sights. If they could do that, his reign of terror would end. If they didn't, he would continue killing again and again and again.

He met her on that hot August morning on Noxon Street, near Soldier's Fountain in the city. She was thirty-three years old. She hailed from Yonkers, a city downstate. Her name was Audrey Pugliese.

"Hi, Audrey," he said brightly on that hot morning.

"Hey, Kendall," she had replied.

They had been together before. She knew the routine.

After negotiating the price for the sex, Francois tooled the car down Main and over to Fulton, taking the left and parking in the garage behind his house. This time, though, they didn't go to the second-floor bedroom as they had before. He took her to the basement instead.

They got undressed and began. In the middle of "making love," Francois flipped. Not flipped over, just flipped his lid. The anger had been building. It was now ready to be unleashed. Strong hands lashed out and the blows found their target on Pugliese's face. She was stunned for a few moments; then she fought back.

Pugliese struggled to get free. She pulled away from him, making for the door. Just when she thought she was out, she got pulled back in. He pulled her around to face him. He punched her, beating her mercilessly around the face and head.

Like some punch-drunk fighter trapped in the corner of the ring, Pugliese must have, involuntarily, covered up. She would have tried to push him off her, struggling, struggling . . . and then she fell to the dirty, cold floor. Francois's foot lashed out like a piston. He stomped her face into a bloody pulp. Shattering ribs, the foot crashed home into her rib cage and stomach. And still, despite the terrible and brutal beating, Audrey Pugliese tried to rise, tried to escape. Her survival sense was in full mode.

If only, if only . . .

His hands clamped down on her neck. She couldn't see them because of the blood in her eyes, but she would have felt him choking the life out of her. She would have been conscious for at least part of the time that she was being killed. How long is hard to tell. Francois had already beaten Pugliese severely; it's doubtful she could have lasted very long.

At last, he heard the throat bone crack. He let her drop like the sack of garbage he considered her to be.

She struggled more than any of the others, he thought, breathing hard.

Francois picked up her limp form and carried her over to the crawl space. He put her on the ledge, then climbed up. Bending down, he pulled her in, depositing her body on top of French's. Then he climbed down and went outside.

It was a nice day. A very nice day.

August 25, 1998

It was the kind of late summer day that locals said was so hot, you could fry eggs on the sidewalk. It was the sidewalk the streetwalker trod day after day.

At only twenty-five years of age, Catina Newmaster was a mother of five. Despite that, despite the responsibilities she had to her children, she continued her self-destructive lifestyle. She really wanted to straighten out her life and be with her kids, but the drugs made that an impossibility.

Catina told her boyfriend, Christopher Briggs, how helpless she was against the drugs. She wanted to kick, but just couldn't.

Poughkeepsie was a long way from the ocean that Catina adored and dreamed about being close to. It was a long way from the beautiful flowers she loved to look at, instead of the fat man who drove up to her on that early morning in his white car.

Catina Newmaster and Kendall Francois knew each other from past sexual encounters. They were old friends, or rather he was an old john of hers. He supplied her with money for her addiction. It was a straight business transaction.

They didn't have to beat around the bush. He told her what he wanted. She told him the price. He agreed. She went around to the passenger-side door and got in. She could smell him. She'd just have to ignore the odor because she needed the money.

For some reason, Kendall didn't like doing it in the car like so many of her other johns. He had to go back to his house. They lost time that way. After all, she was a working girl and on the clock. But he was the client and he made the choice of where to do it. Besides, she needed the money.

Francois drove the few blocks off Main, making the left on Fulton, then down and a left into the alley behind his house. Francois got out and opened the garage door, got back in and drove the car inside. He turned the motor off, then turned to Newmaster and grabbed her.

Newmaster would have felt the fat man's heavy hands on her clothing, pawing, pulling. He pulled her onto him and her panties down.

He opened his pants and took his penis out and started pumping it inside her. They kept going at it, like before. They were getting toward his climax, when Kendall looked up at her with a ferocity she had probably never seen before. His fingers, which before had been playing with her body, albeit roughly, now slid upward to her thin neck.

She ripped me off before, he thought.

He'd felt betrayed then. Now those feelings found their way into his strong hands. He squeezed.

That first moment of panic was probably the worst. Newmaster knew it was more than rough sex. She couldn't breathe and it got worse. His hands kept squeezing her throat and the pain was excruciating. Her hands flailed out, trying to find purchase and failing as her strength ebbed. She collapsed into unconsciousness.

Francois was by now an experienced killer. He kept squeezing until he heard the *snap* of the hyoid bone. When he let go, finally, she collapsed. Looking down at her body on the seat, Francois could see the red imprint of his fingers around her throat.

She was dead. But now, what to do with the body? He decided to carry her inside the house for now. The attic had long been filled up. He would bury her, instead, in the crawl space. Not now, though.

Francois closed the door, locked the car and drew the garage door down. She'd keep till the next morning. Wouldn't do much good to carry her in then. It was broad daylight. There were houses on either side. There was a sidewalk that ran directly in front of the Francois house. Someone might see him; though in his neighborhood, no one ever did.

The following day, August 26, when Senior Investigator Jimmy Ayling reported to work at his Albany office, there was a new name on the screen in his Missing Persons database—Catina Newmaster. After reading the entry, including her occupation, description and the place she had last been seen, on the streets of Poughkeepsie, he knew that the Poughkeepsie Serial Killer had struck again.

Back in Poughkeepsie, about the same time Francois was transferring Newmaster's body from the garage to the crawl space, Bill Siegrist was looking at a hard copy of the Newmaster Missing Person's Report.

Why didn't she listen to me, dammit! If Catina is missing, the same thing happened to her as happened to the others, Siegrist thought.

He hoped she would turn up alive, but doubted it. He was sure—the towheaded child he had befriended had become another victim. He put the paper aside and began thinking about the task force's next move. While he was doing that, across town, Francois finished up the premature burial of Catina Newmaster. Like the cop, Francois wondered, too, what his next move would be.

If it were a baseball game, the score would be "Killer nine, Police and Public, nothing."

Despite what TV network programmers might think, the public is not a group of morons. They watch TV, read papers and magazines. The women were missed. And mourned, especially by their relatives, who believed that they were dead.

The relatives of the missing women had been after the cops to make a concerted effort to find them on the off chance that some might still be alive. Who knew? Maybe the bad guy was like the serial killer "Buffalo Bill" in *The Silence of the Lambs*. "Bill" kept his victims alive until he was ready to skin them and, while the latter was not something to think about, the former was.

The relatives, and the portion of the public that cared, believed that the police had not taken their pleas seriously. The cops, they thought, saw the missing women as a lower order of life because of their profession and drug problems. If the missing women were middle class, you'd see how fast the cops would get the killer, they thought. As a result, the police weren't putting their best effort forward. Of course, nothing was further from the truth.

Siegrist and his brethren wanted to catch the killer in the worst way. They were doing everything they could. All they could hope for was a break, a little piece of luck. And if luck is defined as preparedness meets opportunity, the cops were certainly prepared. Siegrist called up his FBI contact Charley Dorsey to discuss what to do next.

"What do you think, Charley?" Siegrist asked.

They had spoken about the case many times before and the lieutenant valued the G-man's opinion.

"What the fuck can you tell me?" Siegrist asked in obvious exasperation.

"Set up a roadblock on Main Street," Dorsey advised.

A roadblock? That was the kind of ham-fisted policing that did nothing but get motorists angry and rarely yielded results. What killer in his right mind would think to even be in a car traveling through a police checkpoint? Hell, if you just walked on the sidewalk, they wouldn't notice you and you could be on your merry way.

No, Siegrist had precious little to hope for from the Feds, not if you looked back at how ineffectual they had been in the whole investigation. Still, maybe Dorsey's suggestion was worth a try.

Ten

The task force's existence was finally made public. The press and, in turn, the public, was let in on the secret. There were now five cops working full-time, representing three police agencies, to track the killer down.

Commenting in the local press, one former director of the FBI's "elite behavioral sciences unit" maintained that the disappearance of the women was not coincidental. He stated the obvious when he said, "Prostitutes make easy targets." Another former FBI profiler quoted in the same article said essentially the same thing. For the public reading such statements, it sounded like the Federal agents really knew what they were talking about.

They didn't.

The FBI first decided to take a proactive stance against serial killers in 1978. Dr. Maurice Godwin in *Hunting Serial Predators,* his revolutionary text on the subject, writes, "The impetus for the project was to conduct personal interviews with serial murderers about their crimes in order to find out how they were successful at avoiding capture."

According to Godwin, the idea was "to use interviews with convicted killers as the basis for constructing future classifications, which then could be used to aid police investigations." What followed were a series of interviews with 36 convicted offenders, "of whom 25 were defined as serial murderers (i.e., the killing of three or more individuals over time)." Those interviews took place between 1979 and 1983.

The FBI serial murder project was given added attention in Washington, D.C., in the early 1980's due to public outcry over the murder of a six-year-old boy in Florida by a serial murderer. According to Godwin, due to public pressure, the FBI serial murder project was brought to the forefront and given the necessary U.S. government funding, which eventually led to a unit being established in Quantico, Virginia, called the Behavioral Science Unit (BSU).

"The primary purpose of the serial murder project was to use interviews with convicted killers as a basis for constructing future classifications, which then could be used to aid police investigations," wrote Godwin. But the project was founded on a house of cards.

Before questioning, information on each offender and their crimes was obtained through the usual police channels—physical evidence, court transcripts, crime-scene photos, autopsy reports, victim reports, psychiatric reports and prison records. Questions were then together in an unstructured checklist.

What made all of this essentially a house of cards with little or no validity was that according to Godwin, "no detailed analysis of this material has ever been presented. Instead, a simple dichotomy was claimed to emerge from the project by which offenders were classified as either organized or disorganized. The assignment of the offenders to either the organized or disorganized category was based on the appearance of the victim's attire or nudity, the exposure of the victim's sexual parts, the insertion of foreign objects in body cavities, or evidence of sexual intercourse."

The idea, according to the FBI, was to create a major subcategory of serial murderers—sex-related murders *where motive was often lacking*. Therefore, where the murderer was emotional and seemingly disorganized, interpreted from his actions at the crime scene, there was no motive.

"Because of the apparent lack of motive, FBI profilers decided to look for evidence of planning, irrationality or some form of discord at the crime scene in order to determine whether the offender was organized or disorganized. The organized and disorganized typology is then used to classify the murderer's personality, depending on which category the crime scene falls into," wrote Godwin.

In their own literature, the FBI failed to explain the differences between the organized and disorganized serial murderer. Instead, the

FBI classification seems to more fully describe the killer's relative level of aggression when committing murder.

The actual differences between the organized and disorganized crime scenes are explained away by the assailants' psychodynamic drives, which fall into two categories, revenge and sadism. The FBI posits that these drives find their form in "lasting urges" that stem from early childhood experiences. And the latter have been organized around conflict, including defenses, conscience and reality, which butts up against these insatiable drives.

Unfortunately, as early as 1986, researchers specializing in the study of serial murder refuted the FBI classification model. K. A. Busch and J. L. Cavanaugh, writing in the *Journal of Interpersonal Violence* in 1986, stated that the FBI classification model produced statements that were unfounded and not supported by data collection. The FBI case reports on serial murder did not take into consideration contributory factors outside of those already advanced.

In other words, the FBI's theory of serial murder was made to fit each case, regardless of facts. Any police officers asking for help in catching a serial killer in their jurisdiction would get a cookie-cutter profile from the FBI, putting the suspected serial killer into one of these two categories—organized or disorganized.

In terms of specific information that would help the police catch one of these monsters, there was none. In fact, according to Maurice Godwin, there is no example where an FBI profile of a serial killer actually helped in catching one. Worst of all, the two researchers, Busch and Cavanaugh, also concluded that the initial sampling was flawed. Its inherent smallness introduced an element of bias that made all of it inherently unreliable. Why then, with so much valid criticism directed against it, did the FBI have this reputation of tracking down serial killers?

Thomas Harris's 1986 novel about the FBI Behavioral Sciences Unit, *Red Dragon,* first introduced the character of the droll serial killer "Hannibal the Cannibal." It was made into a film in 1987 by director Michael Mann, and retitled *Manhunter,* Brian Cox played the part of "Hannibal."

The serial killer did not receive legendary pop-culture status until Harris's sequel, *The Silence of the Lambs,* was made into the film with the same title in 1991. When Anthony Hopkins took over the "Hannibal" role and won an Oscar for his amazing performance, suddenly serial killers were the bad guys the public wanted to know about. The intrepid FBI agents who could "profile" them and get inside their minds, like Jodie Foster's "Clarice Starling," influenced the public's perception of the bureau and its role in successfully tracking down these fiends. Unfortunately, like so much in popular culture, it had no basis in reality.

By 1995, the bureau had restructured and combined BSU with the Violent Criminal Apprehension Program (ViCAP) and the National Center for the Analysis of Violent Crime. The new unit was called the Critical Incident Response Group (CSIG). The CSIG bases its profiles more upon hunches than science. There are no statistical models to go by. It is, essentially, imitating the dysfunction and lack of validation of its predecessor agency. There was still no empirical research to support the FBI's profiles. That only made Bill Siegrist's job that much harder.

Siegrist, who had turned to the FBI for help in tracking down the Poughkeepsie Serial Killer, was forced to rely on the old organized/disorganized serial killer models. In doing so, he was relying on what amounted to government voodoo.

Maybe the killer was someplace sticking pins into dolls of his victims; Siegrist didn't know. And it didn't matter. He had reports from the FBI that were of no practical value and a killer who had gone to ground and no leads to his identity or whereabouts.

By the morning he talked to Charlie Dorsey again, he was out of options, almost out of hope. That was when Dorsey made his succinct suggestion.

"Set up a roadblock on Main Street," Dorsey said.

Hand out fliers with the girls' pictures on them, suggested Dorsey. They'd be able to look in the cars and see if anyone was being abducted. It might slow "the guy" up. Hopefully, if they cast their net wide enough, they might catch their fish.

Siegrist figured it was worth a try.

* * *

September 2, 1998

The Poughkeepsie Police got out on Main Street early, in time to stop the early morning business traffic. As cars traversed Main Street where it intersected with Church, cops in both lanes stopped traffic. They looked in cars and handed out the fliers with the missing women's pictures on them.

Skip Mannain and Bob McCready from the task force were assigned to street duty. They did a canvass, of the shops on Main Street, asking the storekeepers and passersby if they had seen any of the women.

On the sidewalk, back in the shadows, the hookers watched solemnly. They knew only too well that they could have been on those fliers. It was a strong enough realization to almost sober them up.

Kendall Francois pumped hard inside Diane Franco. She shivered from the force, the pure anger of his stroke. She might have shivered even more if she knew Francois was HIV positive. In addition to everything else, he was a carrier of the deadly disease, which he had probably gotten through the promiscuous sex he engaged in with the prostitutes.

Francois never let any of the women know he was infected. That was their problem. After all, to him they were just whores.

Franco began to feel uncomfortable. He stunk to high heaven. Why didn't the guy take a shower? She couldn't, though, complain very much.

That morning at about eight A.M., Diane Franco had strolled over to a run-down Dunkin' Donuts on Main Street. The sign on the place was broken, but inside the horseshoe counter was active with people getting their morning fill of caffeine and sugar. Before she had even gotten a chance to go inside and get her fix of both, Kendall Francois had pulled to the curb beside her and rolled down the passenger-side window of his white Toyota Camry.

"Want a ride?"

Franco knew Francois from at least one other sexual encounter. She'd been to his house before.

"Sure," she said and got in.

He paid for sex with her. It was all a matter of money, simply a business arrangement. But there was something about Kendall, something Franco just couldn't put her finger on.

Francois drove down Main Street, past the Top Tomato luncheonette and a spanking-new Eckerd's drugstore. It was brilliant marketing— the johns who cruised the area could stop in for some condoms before they picked up the women who cruised the street at all hours of the day and night.

So far, things were going along like clockwork. Franco figured to get through with him, then go back out on Main Street and find some more business. Unlike many of her clients, who preferred cars, Francois had chosen to do it in his house. Actually on the second floor of the house. Looking up at it, Franco thought the place looked kind of old.

Francois and Franco strolled from the garage in the yard in the back of the house, to the side entrance in the alley that separated the house from the one next door. Canvassed later by detectives, all the neighbors told the same story: they saw nothing, they heard nothing.

Inside, Franco wrinkled up her nose at the smell. She couldn't figure out what it was. But why should she be any different? His family still believed that the awful smell was from a family of raccoons that had gotten into the attic where they died. He just hadn't got around to moving all the carcasses yet.

Up the paint-chipped stairs, strewn with garbage, Franco and Francois climbed and off the second-floor landing into Francois's bedroom. Once inside, they got to the matter at hand. It didn't take too long. After they'd finished having sex, Francois would later recall, Diane Franco asked him for her money. They got into an argument over it. His face twisted into a paroxysm of fury. Those hands, that had once pushed opposing wrestlers like so many fleas, quickly closed around Franco's throat. Kendall Francois's powerful hands pressed deep into her flesh. And squeezed.

When he squeezed hard enough, he would break the hyoid bone at the top of her larynx, paralyzing her ability to scream and putting her into shock. That would happen after Francois had squeezed long enough, and hard enough to cut off the oxygen flow to her brain. She'd pass into unconsciousness and from there into death. After that, Francois would then make sure that she was eliminated, that she disappeared like all the rest.

But that day, God was with Diane Franco. How else to explain what happened next?

Franco was a lightweight, all of 5'3" tall and less than 130 pounds soaking wet. She did not work out, she did not eat right and she was known to use drugs. She was not in the best of shape. But she fought with her heart and her soul, with everything she had.

I will not die, her brain seemed to shout to her body.

In a superhuman show of strength, the slight woman broke free from the death grip of the killer. She pushed off the bed and managed to gain her footing.

"Look, why don't we just forget about this?" she said, her head pounding with the blood rushing through it, her legs wobbly from the lack of oxygen to her muscles.

Francois looked at her. Over the next few minutes, Franco made the kind of argument for life that Daniel Webster had made with the Devil. Kendall Francois continued to stare at her, his breath quickening, weighing whether to move in for the kill.

In the end, he decided to let her live. But it wouldn't do for his reputation to have her just walk out the front door of his house and stroll through the late summer sunshine back to Main Street.

Who knows who would see her? Who knew what she might say or do? No, better to keep control of the situation.

"I'll drive you back to Main Street," he volunteered.

They walked down the refuse-filled hallway, down the dirty, garbage-strewn stairwell, down to the first level of the three-level house. Francois opened the side door of the house that led into the alley that separated it from the adjacent house.

No one saw anything. No one heard anything. Francois led her to the white Camry parked inside the detached garage in the rear of the litter-scattered yard. There was a battered, forlorn child's desk next to a tree that had some sort of fungus on its bark.

Franco got in on the front passenger side, while Francois fit his immense bulk behind the wheel. Diane's heart beat wildly. Would she make it back to Main Street alive or would he detour to somewhere else and finish the job? Sure, he said he was going to take her back to Main Street. He might do that, but didn't he just try to kill her?

Kendall Francois backed his car down the driveway and out onto Fulton Avenue. He passed a red Trans Am parked at the curb across the street.

As he drove slowly down the street, Franco noticed the doctors' office right next door to Francois's home, the neat one-family houses that dotted the street. Some were Cape Cods, some Colonials, one or two ranches and, of course, the older Victorians, which is what the Francois house was. Signs warned not to park November 1 through April 1 from twelve to eight A.M. No way the residents wanted any of the Main Street scum of prostitution, crime and drugs filtering over in their direction.

NEIGHBORHOOD WATCH AREA another sign emphasized. That one should have amused Francois.

The Neighborhood Watch was a community-policing program in which residents kept a sharp eye out for anything out of the ordinary. If anything did happen that shouldn't, if anyone saw something suspicious, the idea was to report it to the police immediately. Yet, not one call had come into the police about Francois.

Not one.

The sign to the contrary, it was not unlike other insular neighborhoods in the country that try mightily to keep out those who might intrude on the residents' privacy, yet never consider that the menace could come from within.

Vassar College was two more blocks down, but Francois swung the car to the left at the corner and headed back to Main Street. It was just two more blocks, Franco realized.

They had just passed Top Tomato. She looked at the car door. She hadn't locked it. Then she looked over at the big black man behind the wheel who, moments before, had almost strangled her to death and thought about what could still happen.

"How about over there?" said Diane Franco to Kendall Francois.

She pointed to the left, to a Sunoco station on the corner of Main and Grand. Dutifully, Francois pulled off to the left. The Camry's fourteen-inch wheels had just climbed the curb when Franco broke for freedom.

Franco threw open the passenger-side door and ran. Unless he wanted to attract a crowd, which surely he did not, Francois had to let her go. He watched her run away as he turned and drove back in the opposite direction.

"There's Kendall," said Mannain to Mc-Cready.

Mannain had been investigating the disappearance of the Poughkeepsie street women since the first one was reported on October 24, 1996. Another month and it would be the two-year anniversary, two years without a suspect's arrest, two years of killing after killing. Skip Mannain was the only member of the task force who had been on the case since the beginning. It seemed like ages ago.

They were still handing out fliers when they saw the big man's white Camry coming off the gas station lot on Grand and Main, proceeding in the opposite direction. Mannain waved and Francois, returning the friendly gesture with a wave of his own, drove on by and disappeared around the corner.

"Let's pull in," Mannain suggested.

He drove his car into the same gas station Francois had just come from. After pulling in, they heard a man screaming. It was Jim Meadows, an employee of the Sunoco gas station.

Calmly, Mannain reached into his jacket pocket and pulled out his wallet. He flipped it open. Inside on the left flap was an identification card. On the right was a shiny badge that said DETECTIVE, CITY OF POUGHKEEPSIE.

"A woman just ran in the station claiming she'd been raped," said the gas jockey, sticking his head in the front passenger window.

"What's her name?" Mannain asked.

"Her name's Diane Franco."

"Where is she?"

Meadows looked around. After a moment, he spotted Franco, about a half block distant, walking slowly.

"There." He pointed.

Mannain tooled the car off the curb and drove quickly down Main Street, easily overtaking Franco. He turned in and parked a few feet in front of her. Car doors slammed and the cops were instantly on the curb. They flashed their badges.

"I'm Detective Mannain of the city police," said Mannain, and then he introduced his partner. "We just heard from a man at the gas station that you were assaulted."

Franco was hesitant. After a moment, she said there was nothing she wanted to report. Mannain was perplexed. She'd just been attacked and didn't want to report it?

"She thought there was a warrant out for her," Siegrist would later explain. "That's why she didn't want to report the rape and assault."

Mannain wouldn't let her say "No."

"You have to come with us," Mannain told her. "Come on, if someone hurt you, you can't let them get away with it. They might do it to somebody else. You know what's going on out here."

Franco certainly did. After a few moments, she acquiesced and agreed to come on in and talk. Since the alleged assault had occurred in Francois's house, which was in the town of Poughkeepsie, a mere three feet from the imaginary border that separated it from the city of Poughkeepsie, Franco was brought to the Town of Poughkeepsie Police Headquarters.

McCready found a vacant interview room. They made her as comfortable as they could and reassured her that they were only interested in the man who had assaulted her. Once they had gained her trust, they interviewed her.

Prostitutes don't generally like to charge customers with being too rough. It's a matter of business. Do that and they'd never come back. But Francois was different; it was like he *meant* it. Besides, the cops seemed sincere in their desire to bring the big guy in.

"Do you know who did it?" Mannain asked.

"Yeah, Kendall Francois."

Mannain felt the hairs on the back of his neck prick up. It was the kind of feeling that a good cop gets when he knows he is at the end of a long hunt. But they had been down this road before with Francois—he already had two misdemeanor convictions for activities relating to solicitation. They needed to go by the book.

Mannain wanted her to file a complaint against Francois. Without that, their hands would be tied and they'd be right back where they were, except it was two years later and still no one in custody.

A short while later, the phone rang in Siegrist's office. He picked it up off the cradle.

"Lieutenant Siegrist."

"Bill, it's Skip."

The junior man sounded excited. He quickly explained what had happened.

It's Kendall again, thought Siegrist.

"And you got the girl to file a complaint?" Siegrist asked.

"Yes," Mannain answered. "The town's picking him up now."

"Keep me informed," said Siegrist.

Siegrist went back to work. They had been down this road before. Only if they got a search warrant to search the house did he expect anything to appreciably change.

Eleven

Once again, jurisdiction was important.

The Francois house was located in the town of Poughkeepsie, not the city of Poughkeepsie. It was in the town where the alleged assault against Franco had occurred. Accordingly, it was Detective Sergeant Daniel Lundgren and Detective Jon Wagner of the town police who drove over to Fulton Avenue to make the arrest.

The doors of the unmarked police car slammed in the early afternoon sunshine. The cops could hear the birds in the trees chirping as they climbed the rickety wooden steps. At the top, they found themselves on a weathered wooden porch strewn with garbage.

Francois heard the knock. After a moment, Francois answered and came out to talk with them. The time, Lundgren would later note, was three P.M.

"I'm Detective Sergeant Daniel Lundgren and this is my partner, Detective Jon Wagner, of the town police," said Lundgren, flashing his badge. "Would you come to the police department with us please?"

Francois looked at the two men emotion-lessly.

"Sure," he said easily.

Without arguing or struggling, Francois read-ily agreed. He got into the police car and was driven downtown for their little chat.

Once they arrived at police headquarters, they showed Kendall Francois to Room 112, an interview room not unlike any other in the building—a medium-size rectangle with a desk in the middle and a group of chairs around it. The walls were painted institutional green. The place smelled from stale coffee, cigarettes, sweat and desperation.

At four P.M., McCready and Mannain came in to talk to Francois. The first thing they did was advise him of his Miranda rights.

"You have the right to remain silent. Any-thing you say can and will be used against you in a court of law. You have the right to the presence of an attorney. If you cannot afford one, one will be appointed by the court. Do you understand these rights?"

Francois said that he did.

"Do you wish to speak with us without an attorney being present?"

That was the crucial question. If Francois said no and invoked his constitutional right to have an attorney present, the interview was over.

"No, I'll speak to you without an attorney," Francois said.

Surely, Francois had seen any number of cop shows on television where the Miranda warning

was recited. He knew that talking would only
lead to further incarceration. Implicating himself in Franco's assault or something even more
serious, like murder, was a stupid thing to do.
But no one ever said that criminals were
smarter than most people. If they were, they
would never be caught.

Mannain knew they had gotten a break. The
last time when they'd questioned Francois, he'd
lawyered up. There'd be plenty of time to wonder why he hadn't this time. For a change, the
cops had the opportunity for a little chat.

"Okay, Kendall," said McCready, "we want to
speak with you about a person you were with
earlier this morning."

"Diane Franco," said Mannain casually.

"Allegedly, you assaulted her during a sexual
encounter at your home," McCready continued.

"Well, I paid to have sex with her," Francois
admitted. "I didn't sexually assault her in any
manner."

"Ms. Franco was very detailed in her complaint. And I noticed she had marks around
her neck, like someone had tried to strangle
her," said McCready.

"Okay, I choked her, but," he tried to explain, "we were having sex—"

"Intercourse?" asked Mannain.

"Yes," said Francois.

"Where were you?"

"In my car inside the garage at my house.
We were having sex in my car inside the garage
at my house when we got into an argument."

"Then what happened?"

"I got angry and grabbed her by the throat. We continued having sex. And I began choking her with my hands."

There was silence in the room. They still didn't have enough. What they had was a co-incidence. They needed to make it stick. They really needed the bodies to charge him. With-out a corpse, convicting a man of murder is almost impossible. It rarely happens.

"Did you calm down?" McCready asked, knowing full well that he had.

Francois nodded.

"So what happened after you calmed down?" McCready continued.

"After I calmed down, well, I, uh, we contin-ued having sex."

"What happened when you were finished?"

"I drove her to a gas station on Main Street and dropped her off."

The cops knew that once a suspect was given his Miranda warning, and continued to talk without a lawyer present, the more he talked to police, the better chance more details would come out to pin him to the crime being inves-tigated. In most cases, it was through circum-stantial evidence and physical evidence, like DNA found at the crime scene, that was then matched to the suspect that ultimately led to a conviction.

In rare instances, the suspect actually con-fessed. That could also be thrown out later on various constitutional grounds, which was why it was always useful to have the physical evidence.

Bearing that in mind, Franco had filed charges against Francois. She was then taken to a local hospital where a rape kit was used. A piece of her hair was carefully snipped and placed in an evidence bag. Likewise, swabs from inside her vagina. Those swabs held the semen from her assailant and in turn, the semen held the malefactor's DNA code.

The police were hopeful that Francois might say something so incriminating that they could use it to get a court order demanding that Francois turn over samples of his saliva, hair and blood. Lab specialists would then crack his DNA code from those samples and attempt to match it up to the DNA code from the semen taken from Franco's vagina.

A match would confirm Franco's story. That, coupled with the bruises on her neck, which police were certain matched Francois's hands, could lead to a rape conviction and, perhaps, a search warrant to search the house for further evidence. Of course, there would be no guarantee of conviction, even with hard evidence.

Most people looked at prostitutes as being a lower order of life, not subject to the same protection given to most. At trial, the jury might figure the woman really consented and things got out of control. In that case, they could convict on a lesser charge than rape, maybe even find Francois not guilty, in which case he would walk.

They continued to talk. There was a lot to talk about.

Back in his office, Bill Siegrist looked at his watch. Five o'clock. He had an appointment and didn't want to be late.

Siegrist had been planning on putting a new roof on his twenty-six-year-old house for the past two years. Although it was only early September, he knew from years past that winter comes fast to the Hudson Valley. One day it could be fall, with the air sharp, cool and comfortable, and the next, literally overnight, winter could set in. There were years with frosts in late September.

So he needed to get the roof done once and for all and while he was at it, it was also time to get some changes made to the house's structure. To do all that, he had hired local architect Doug Hughes.

Siegrist drove out of town, going east on the side streets. He wanted to avoid the inevitable Church Street traffic until he was farther out of the city, into the township. Then he turned back onto Church, technically Route 55, and continued heading east. He passed a few strip malls and then scattered sections of rolling farmland.

Siegrist made his home with his wife, Liz, and his children eight miles outside of town in Pleasant Valley. It was as bucolic as the name implied—a stark contrast to the urban chaos of the cop's working environment.

When Siegrist got home, he found Liz waiting for him in the backyard. They chatted for a bit, gazing up at the roof and noting its poor condition. It really did need replacing. Just then the doorbell rang. The couple made their way through the house's interior, out to the front door.

"Hi, Doug," said Siegrist as he opened the door.

It was the architect Hughes, come to get final approval on his plans.

"Let's go into the dining room," said Siegrist, leading the way.

After exchanging small talk, Hughes laid his blueprints down on the dining room table. Carefully, he unrolled them. The Siegrists gazed at the blueprints. They were very satisfied with what they saw. They liked Hughes's work. He understood exactly what needed to be done. Nodding, Siegrist reached up and unbuttoned the top button of his shirt. Then he pulled at his tie, lowering it a little.

With pen in hand, he reached down to initial the plans. It would be the final go-ahead for construction. Then, just before his pen touched the paper, the phone rang. Siegrist was annoyed.

"I'll get it," Siegrist said to his wife. He strode back up to the kitchen, where he picked the receiver off the wall.

In some localities, it is standard practice to take down the first interview longhand, the sec-

ond on tape. The town of Poughkeepsie was
such a locality.

A little before 4:38 P.M., Francois was once
again advised of his Miranda rights. Once
again, he waived them. Mannain was tense.

When Francois began talking a second time,
a tape recorder, which had been brought into
the room, was turned on to record his every
word. McCready and Mannain then asked him
to repeat the details of his day, how he happened to meet Diane Franco and to tell them
again what happened.

"This morning at about eight-thirty A.M.," he
began, "I was downtown."

"Where?" McCready asked.

"In the vicinity of Pershing Avenue," Francois answered and the cops knew that was part
of the neighborhood where prostitutes hung
out on the street waiting for johns to pick them
up.

"I was driving alone in my car."

"The Camry?"

"Yes. I stopped and spoke with Diane Franco.
I knew her."

It seemed that Franco and Francois had
transacted business on a few prior occasions.

"She agreed to have sex with me for money."

Franco got into the Camry and Francois
drove over to his house. He didn't have an
automatic garage-door opener. He got out and,
by hand, opened the door, painted with old
gray paint that was chipped and faded.

"I drove the car into the garage, got out and
closed it [the door]."

When he got back in, he gave Franco, in advance, money to have sexual intercourse with him. They did it on the front seat of the car. After a while of his pounding into her, of his massive weight bearing down on the slight prostitute's body, she said, "I want to stop."

Francois wouldn't. He'd paid and he was going to get everything that was his entitlement. They had a disagreement. Franco wasn't going to give it up. They argued. Francois blew his top.

"I got angry and grabbed her around the neck, started to choke her with my hands."

Somehow he managed to calm down before he did any permanent physical damage. They went on to have sex again. The tape recorder was turned off.

The brief tape-recorded questioning had produced a little more in the way of detail. Most detectives would have continued questioning him, because they clearly did not have enough to charge him with anything other than rape. That was a minor charge compared to nine counts of murder.

Maybe the cops were psychic and figured there was no need to press. Maybe they were so intuitive they knew what would happen next. Or maybe it was just blind luck. What happened was that after the questioning Francois was left alone in Interview Room 112. After a while, he called out that he wanted to see the two officers who had been in the room with him. Mannain and McCready went in.

"I'd like to talk to a prosecutor," said Kendall Francois. "I want to look at the photos of prostitutes missing since 1993."

1993? The cops had only been concerned with the women missing since 1996. Were there *more*? And why did Francois want to discuss the missing women, unless he knew something?

In police work, it's best not to jump to conclusions. Without further analysis, a call was placed to the on-call prosecutor, Dutchess County Assistant District Attorney Marjorie J. Smith. Her job, during her shift, in addition to her regular work, was to assist cops in putting together cases. She was summoned from her office on Main Street. So was task force member Arthur Boyko of the state police.

Francois was shown a series of Web-site photos of women whose pictures appeared on official Missing Person's reports. Methodically, Francois flipped through the papers and carefully separated them out. He placed four photos in one pile. Mannain looked down at the pictures.

In one pile, Francois had placed pictures of Wendy Meyers, Gina Barone, Catherine Marsh and Sandra French.

"I killed them," said Kendall Francois.

Mannain looked up sharply.

"What?"

"I killed them."

Holy shit!

The last thing he expected was for the guy to cop to the murders. The big man placed photos of Michelle Eason and Kathleen Hurley aside.

"I don't know about them."

He looked at the Web-site photo of Mary Healey Giaccone.

"I'm not sure about her either."

Kendall Francois then continued with his statement.

At the Siegrist house, the phone rang. Annoyed, Siegrist picked it up.

"Hello?" said the lieutenant of detectives.

"Bill, get over here!" It was Skip Mannain and he sounded excited. "Get your fucking ass over here!"

"Skip, what—"

"He's going for it."

"He's *what?*"

"He's going for it," Mannain repeated. "He's drawing maps!"

Siegrist gripped the phone harder. "Oh, my God."

"Get your fucking ass over here!"

"I'll be right there."

Quickly, Siegrist slung the receiver back in the cradle and, in almost the same motion, pivoted and strode quickly out into the dining area. Liz and Doug looked at him expectantly.

"I gotta go," he said to his wife, kissing her quickly on the cheek.

Liz was used to this behavior, but the architect wasn't. He watched quizzically as the cop went out the front door. Before he left, Siegrist pushed his tie up and buttoned his shirt.

Outside, Siegrist was in his unmarked car in

a flash. He reached down under his seat and brought up a domed light, which he attached to the roof of the Taurus. He gunned the motor to life, then spun around hard and out the driveway. Hitting Route 55 going west, he turned on his siren. Suddenly, traffic parted like the Red Sea. Siegrist didn't really notice any of that. When one's mind is extremely active, it can perform two tasks at the same time—for instance, driving and thinking about a murder case.

Siegrist could see how and where he was going, but his mind projected forward four miles, to the Town of Poughkeepsie Police Station. It was there, in an interview room, that Kendall Francois was talking. Finally.

Be careful what you wish for, you might get it, goes the old proverb. Siegrist and company had wanted to know what had happened to the missing women. Now, maybe, that was finally happening.

Holy shit, thought Siegrist, hands swiftly negotiating the wheel. If he's drawing maps, we may be up in the woods all night. The detective lieutenant expected that Francois was confessing that he'd killed the women and buried them somewhere in the woods outside town. To Siegrist, that made sense.

Nice remote location, maybe nobody finds them. Had to be something like that. Where else could he put that many people?

Siegrist was very excited and few things did that for him. His son's graduation from college was one. But this case, the agony over it and

to see it come to a satisfactory conclusion . . .
As he drove, Siegrist continued to turn the case
over in his mind.

Siegrist figured that Francois had finally decided to confess "because the jig was up." With
a warrant to get into the house, all would become clear very soon. It was actually a practical
matter to confess. Perhaps he could hope for
some sort of leniency with his cooperation.

The last thing Siegrist or anyone else close
to the case figured Francois for was a conscience. If he had one, he wouldn't have racked
up a kill total greater than Jack the Ripper's.

Serial murder is actually a very rare crime.
You have as much of a chance of being a victim
of a serial murderer as winning the lottery. It
is a metaphor that would not comfort any of
the women, but it is true nevertheless.

For those in law enforcement, the opportunity, therefore, to be involved in a serial murder
investigation is rare. Some of the assembled
cops and the prosecutor had been involved on
the periphery of the White serial murder case
many years before. None of the cops, though,
had been the primary officers involved in such
a case.

Once Francois had started talking, he kept
going. With little prompting, the big guy began
to tell the cops exactly where to look. It was
late, of course, too late to help the women who
had been his victims. Closure, though, was possible for their families. Discovering and identi-

fying their bodies would do exactly that. Then there was one more job they had to do.

Death. Everyone hoped for one more death out of the case. New York State had the death penalty, recently reinstated by the state legislature and Governor Pataki. The idea now was to put as strong a case together as possible so the prosecutor could seek the death penalty against Kendall Francois. The more he talked, the more he plunged the executioner's needle loaded with poison into his arm.

Everyone in the room knew that. It was doubtful any of them wanted the big man to stop.

Twelve

Route 44 winds its way out of Poughkeepsie, stretching all the way to the New York–Connecticut border thirty miles away. But you don't have to travel that far to get to Troop K of the New York State Troopers.

Troop K's headquarters is a low-lying, oblong building that sits on an unprepossessing lot in the suburban town of Millbrook. Millbrook and its surrounding towns are like what Long Island is to New York City—a stretch of suburban towns from which the workers that man Poughkeepsie's offices commute every day. What makes Troop K unique, though, is that it serves four of the surrounding counties, as far south as Westchester. That's a lot of area to cover.

For Tommy Martin, autumn, and the days leading up to it, was the perfect time for business. It was cool and generally dry, perfect weather for processing crime scenes. Tommy was the senior investigator in Troop K's Forensic Identification Unit. Only thirty-one, he had been there for ten years.

Late on the evening of September 2, as Kendall Francois was concluding his statement to police, Tommy Martin was relaxing in his home, in a town just a few minutes from Troop K in Millbrook. It was sometime around midnight when the phone rang. His wife, used to such nocturnal summonses, simply turned over in bed as Tommy picked up the receiver.

On the other end was Kevin Rosa, Tom's forty-year-old partner. He had come on the unit in 1995, and held the rank of investigator. It was his first day back from a wonderful late summer vacation and he had decided to stay late that night to catch up on paperwork. He was looking at some slides of a crime scene he had helped process not too long before when a call came in from the Town of Poughkeepsie Police.

"Guess what, they got the guy," Rosa told a still-sleepy Martin.

"What?"

"I said they got the guy, Tommy. The Poughkeepsie Police. They got the guy that strangled those girls. He gave a statement."

"What?"

Tommy Martin didn't believe his partner. Rosa was a clever practical joker.

"I don't believe you," Martin continued. "I'm staying right here."

"This is for real," Rosa answered.

Holy moley, Martin thought. *Even Kevin wouldn't take a joke this far.*

"They want us at the town [police headquarters]."

"Meet you over there," said Martin.

He hung up the phone.

The case may have been unusual, but the call

wasn't. In the Hudson Valley, when local police needed a forensic specialist, the call always went out to Tommy Martin.

Tommy, as everyone who knew him called him, had started out as a road trooper. His primary job had been to keep the roads safe and, of course, give out tickets for speeding. But none of that was satisfying. He began volunteering his services as an extra set of eyes and hands and, most importantly, brains to process crime scenes. While his broad shoulders and blond hair made him look like the archetype of the stupid college jock, appearance, as it so often is, was deceiving.

Martin might have looked like a fullback, but he had the mind of a college professor. He also doubled as one at night at Columbia Greene Community College up in Greene County. Martin had taken his criminology degree at Albany State College, where he received a B.S. in criminal justice. During the day, he processed crime scenes.

Seeing his potential when he first started on the force, his superiors had decided to allow him to put his inquisitive mind to good use. He began with simple burglaries, working his way up to fatal car accidents. Whenever the forensic investigators needed help beyond their staff allotment of personnel, the call went out for Tommy and he was only too glad to answer it. Eventually, he was promoted out of uniform and became a full-time forensics investigator in 1992.

Since that time, forensic science had made

many advances, not the least of which was the now common practice of identifying a suspect through his genetic fingerprint, DNA. But no matter how far science had come, there was still a human being out there physically gathering the evidence to analyze.

Sometimes, Tommy was called in on cases that really weren't crimes. It could be some sort of car accident where it wasn't clear how the accident was caused. It might be a man who died from carbon monoxide poisoning while sitting in his car in his garage and whose wife found him with the motor running.

Was it suicide or murder?

Tommy Martin had the luxury of being called in when there was a crime scene to process. His whole contribution lay in his ability to interpret hard and fast things one could touch, like guns and knives, sinews and blood, skin and bone. Tommy didn't have to worry about tracking down the "bad guy." Tommy didn't have to worry about talking to the victims' families. Tommy didn't even have to deal directly with scumbag murderers. What he did was give the district attorney the palpable evidence to convict felons.

In other words, Tommy Martin didn't discriminate. He was a scientist with a conscience. He was a modern version of the Old West tracker. Like his Old West counterpart, Martin tracked outlaws, except he did it scientifically by processing crime scenes.

Tommy had done a lot of crime scenes. He couldn't remember how many. Thousands, probably. It seemed like he was always busy. Since Troop K serviced four of the largest counties in the state, he was just as apt to be called in on a case in wealthy Westchester County or in the more rural Dutchess County, which was where he got the call on the Francois case.

Despite all his experience, the Francois case would be unusual for Martin. His hard work on it would eventually lead to the most dramatic scene in the history of New York jurisprudence, stretching back over two hundred years to the dawn of the republic.

Less than a half hour after getting the call to get to work, Tommy Martin strolled into the lobby of the Town of Poughkeepsie Police Headquarters. Martin had been through this routine many times before. He knew the procedure before they could get into a suspect's house. The idea was to stage your troops before going into battle.

Martin said, "We applied for warrants to search the house. The idea is to wait for your ducks to line up," so that no court could ever throw out evidence seized in an unconstitutional search.

By one A.M., the assistant district attorney had found a judge to sign a search warrant. They now had a legal right to enter Kendall Francois's home and search for evidence of murder. Martin and Rosa piled into their unmarked 1995 Chevy van and began the short drive to

Fulton Avenue. By the time they got to the Francois home, the city and town cops were already there.

"The first thing you do is set up the crime-scene tape," Martin explained. "You establish a perimeter around the crime scene, in this case the Francois house."

The two state forensic specialists began that process, stringing the tape directly around the house from the curb and all the way around into the yard and back again. While they were doing that, the detectives knocked on the door of the house.

"Yes?" asked the man who answered the door. His name was McKinley Francois. A factory worker, he was Kendall's father.

"Mr. Francois, we're detectives," they said, flashing their badges, "and we've got a warrant to search the premises."

McKinley Francois had no time to be confused. The police hustled him and his wife, Paulette, and their grown daughter Kierstyn out of the house. This was a situation where the needs of the many outweighed the needs of the few. The constitutional right of the state to search the premises for evidence of murder far outweighed the privacy rights that the Francois family were entitled to.

It was nothing personal. Where the family would go, what they would do, was not the state's problem. Besides, they wouldn't be out on the street. Family and friends could take them in. There was probably some provision in their homeowner's insurance policy that would pay for shelter. If not, the county could always find something for them.

What it came down to was this: once the police verified there were bodies in the house, through Francois's statements, which they felt to be true, access to the house was restricted. It had to be, in order for Tommy Martin to do his job. The evidence had to be as pristine as possible so the state could get a conviction.

As for the Francois family, they had to face a basic question: where could they now go? The police had legally kicked them out of their house, the house Paulette and Nat *owned*, in the middle of the night.

After the police dispossessed them, Nat, Paulette and Kierstyn decided to stay with Raquelle, the family's oldest daughter, who had her own place in another part of the city. And as Kendall Francois's loved ones tried to absorb the enormity of what was happening, the sun came up and the detectives continued their work.

Too many homicide cases in the United States have been compromised because of shoddy crime-scene management. In the worst-case scenarios, this shoddy police work allows the guilty to go free. The innocent can wind up being punished.

The most important thing in a homicide investigation is restricting access to the crime scene. Period. If done really professionally, that means that only crime-scene specialists will pro-

cess the crime scene. At the Francois house
that's exactly what happened.

"The first piece of crime-scene tape sur-
rounds the property," Tommy explained.
"Then we rope off the middle of the block"
to further restrict access. "What we are doing
is establishing an inside perimeter and outside
perimeter to the house."

The police officers manning the perimeters
wore different uniforms. Because the outside
perimeter was in the city of Poughkeepsie, that
was the uniform those cops wore. Their coun-
terparts, on the inside perimeter where the
house was, wore the blues of the Town of
Poughkeepsie Police Department.

What no one dared talk about was that conflict might have compromised the investigation.
It had taken a long time to establish the joint
task force, too long, many both in and outside
government felt. Finding the bodies, bringing
closure to the affected families, would go a
long way toward resolution.

Tommy Martin looked up at the Victorian
house. It looked ominous in the darkness. But
he had a job to do. They were going to find
the bodies inside and make the case against the
son of a bitch.

*It's the perfect time of year, not too hot, not too
cold,* thought Tommy Martin as he changed
into his suit.

The neighbors, who had already been roused
by the intense police presence outside, flocked
to their windows. Scattered lights went on all

through the block. Neighbors came out on their stoops and began talking to the uniforms.

"What's going on?"

The cops, taciturn at first, not sure what they could say, just said it was an investigation. But soon, it became evident. The cops were there to look at the house of the guy they suspected had killed nine prostitutes.

"It's the Francoises' house."

"Yeah, that place smelled bad!"

You could hear the comments up and down the street. The police, meanwhile, spoke amongst themselves in quiet, almost reverential tones. They knew the grim business in front of them and had respect for it.

The crowd hushed when they saw what happened next. The cowardly ones peering out from behind closed shades, the more courageous out on the street, saw the doors to the unmarked Ford Chevy van open. Out came two men dressed in Tyvek space suits. Inside those suits were Tommy Martin and Kevin Rosa.

The suits the forensic specialists wore did resemble space suits. They were white and fit from head to toe, with helmets. Full, knee-length boots completed the otherworld effect.

"They're actually Tyvek Coveralls," Martin explained, "sterile suits that keep biohazards from getting on us. See, it's easy to contaminate a crime scene. Like, you bend over to cut out a swatch of carpet that you think has blood on it and your head drips sweat onto it. Even saliva. We all spray a little when we talk."

That wouldn't do. The specialists' fluids con-

taminating the scene could lead to evidence being compromised and ultimately, an innocent
verdict. Martin walked slowly up the driveway,
gauging his surroundings. As he got closer to
the side door of the house, the odor almost
overpowered him.

"I could smell death, walking up that driveway," he said.

The crime-scene specialist took out his flashlight and thumbed it on. The powerful beam
struck out, illuminating the darkness. As Martin
entered the side door of the house, going into
the basement, he noticed a battered clothes
dryer on his right.

"There was a bunch of shit in that basement.
It was loaded with crap."

There was a rusty bicycle that had seen better
days. Off to the right was the furnace and, beyond that, a bookshelf. Then there was an over-
turned chair, its green paint chipping. An old
baby stroller stood off to the side. Francois actually had a brother who was a graduate of
Syracuse University and another sister, neither
of whom lived at home. Maybe one of them
had been in that carriage. Or maybe Francois
himself, when he was a baby.

Back in the very rear of the basement was a
crawl space that looked like a ledge, about five
feet above the ground. Under it was a small
wooden chair. Martin paused. His colleague
Rosa had come up beside him. As one, they
had shone their lights up into the crawl space.

What they saw in the harsh light were two
objects that were covered with a black plastic

bag. Or maybe they were inside the bag. It was hard to be sure. They needed to go in to be certain. But they couldn't, at least not yet, as much as they wanted to.

"You can't hop in and pull off the plastic," Martin explained. "That would destroy evidence."

Martin shone his light again on the bag. That was when he saw something protruding out of the bag, at the top. At first glance, he had missed it, missed it because "it was abstract, seeing it out of human context.

"It was a knee. Someone's knee."

What Martin and Rosa were looking at was a knee, or what had once been one. The skin hung in dark brown ribbons. The tendons had not thoroughly decomposed yet. The skin was just barely there and under it, in all its engineering complexity, was the knee joint, looking bone white in the ghostly light.

Whoever this woman was, she had been there for some time. She didn't look lonely though. The bag looked as though it contained not one, but two bodies. Spraying his light out farther, Martin saw the second object, closer to him than the first. It, too, looked like it was a giant plastic bag, filled up with bones.

The cops had already established that there were bodies in the basement. They had known to look there because Kendall Francois had told them, hours before in the interrogation room, that the crawl space in the basement was where he had unceremoniously dumped some of them. The attic was next.

Breathing shallowly through their space suits, Martin and Rosa withdrew from the basement and climbed the stairs that led to the main story of the house. Neither man felt any anxiety. This was business as usual to them. They were professionals. In some way, they could close off their brains to the tragedy they were witnessing—the end of people's lives, people with hopes and dreams like they had.

"We 'do' a lot of natural deaths and suicides," says Martin, "where the cause of death is initially in doubt until we investigate. So when we work a crime scene, we're used to seeing bodies all the time."

On the first-floor landing, the specialists went through a doorway and into the kitchen. It was dirty, grungy, and disgusting.

Dirt was everywhere, the ancient linoleum blackened from it. Garbage, plastic bottles, half-eaten food in plates had been dumped everywhere. The sink was piled high with dirty dishes.

Over the filthy stove, someone had placed a rack of store-bought dried spices. Martin couldn't even imagine, nor did he want to, what culinary masterpieces might have been created in this pigsty.

They would search the rest of the house further later on. It was getting late and they needed to get into the attic. That was where they expected their next major discoveries to be. They walked up the inside stairs and found themselves on a second-floor landing. Martin noticed that the house was in such dilapidated condition that some of the beams were exposed. The house had a rosewood foundation, which under other circumstances could be made to look beautiful.

They opened a small door cut into the wall. Inside, Martin climbed up a flight of stairs that led to the attic. Once at the top, he didn't step into the room. Again, he needed to take a look around first before he destroyed any evidence. Slowly, methodically, the flashlight beam circled the room, picking up old pieces of furniture and bags, scanning, scanning—

This time, it was more obvious. Lying over there in a corner.

"On the right, near the top, was a clear plastic bag and inside were the skeletal remains, I could see, of at least one person. I couldn't then tell how many might be inside."

But they were skeletons and, even from a distance, safe to say human skeletons. Which, of course, meant they had been there for quite some time. Otherwise, decomposition wouldn't have been so far along.

"The body or bodies were partially in and out of the bag, which he'd put into one of those hard-plastic, kiddy swimming pools," remembered Martin, who took Polaroids of all the bodies.

It was too early to tell if what they were looking at was the actual crime scene. Maybe Francois had killed them someplace else and transported them here. A forensic analysis of the place would answer that question. But for now, what they had was a scene striking for its lack of drama.

There was no blood. There was no weapon. There were no signs of a struggle. There were no signs of any crime for that matter. Just a dirty crawl space, except for one little thing.

What used to be human beings had been stashed in the attic and crawl space of the Francois home.

By the time, Martin and Rosa left the house, Siegrist was already on the scene and up to speed. Martin showed him the Polaroids of the remains. Siegrist looked at them with seeming dispassion.

"Yes, he did it," said Martin quietly. He knew the cops had been on the case since almost the beginning and had a huge stake in its outcome.

Siegrist remembers the tension suddenly draining out of his body. It was like a toxin that had polluted his entire system. Once, it was there. Now, finally, after two years, it was gone.

Bill Siegrist felt very, very tired, like somebody who's just had a great workout. He felt good because now the police had a sense of closure to the case.

While the crime-scene specialists were doing their job, the detectives were doing theirs. They had searched the more obvious regions of the house, including Francois's second-floor bedroom and come up with some damning evidence, which they had placed in evidence envelopes, which were carefully catalogued. Among the things on the list of items confiscated from the house, Siegrist saw the following:

- Audrey Pugliese's driver's license
- A pack of condoms found under a coffee table
- Francois's Dutchess County Community College identification card
- A list of courses the college was offering for the fall 1998 semester
- A leather necklace
- A box of color film

The most damning piece of evidence, Siegrist knew, was Pugliese's driver's license. If Francois didn't kill her, how did it come to be inside his house? For his part, Mannain, who had also arrived, had something he had to do.

Skip Mannain had been on the case for the full two years, longer than anyone else had. He had seen the investigation through all its highs and lows, mostly lows, until Francois confessed. But the confession, or statement as it's called in the trade, does not stop the investigation from continuing.

In addition to the investigation by the forensic team headed up by Martin and Rosa, in coming days, detectives would begin interviewing all of Francois's known acquaintances, backtracking his movements, trying to put together as strong a case as possible. In the event there was a constitutional challenge to his confession, they needed to be prepared with concrete evidence to prosecute him.

But that evening, Mannain had a much grimmer duty than mere investigation. While the women in the attic had not yet been identified, he needed to contact the next of kin of the missing women and tell them what was up before the media swarmed all over the story. It was the only humane thing to do.

Thirteen

At ten P.M., Patricia Barone's evening was interrupted by a knock at the door. It was Mannain, with news of her daughter Gina.

"We think we found her," said Mannain, who sketched in the details. Apparently, Barone wasn't surprised.

"I told Skip [months ago], once we find one, we're going to find them all and we're going to find them right here. Right under our noses," she later said.

By morning, others in her circle knew what had happened.

"Everybody's saying, 'My God, you're holding up.' I mourned my daughter for a long time. It's not like it was yesterday."

Back at headquarters, Mannain picked up the phone and called Albany to speak with Marguerite Marsh, Cathy Marsh's mother.

"The authorities there [in Poughkeepsie] called me and told me my daughter may be one of the women they found in his house. They wanted to prepare me, but haven't positively identified her yet," she would later tell a local paper. "It's been hard and the waiting has been very hard, and now we still have to wait to hear and this is even harder."

What Marsh did not know was that her daughter and Francois had both attended Dutchess County Community College at the same time. At times, they had probably passed each other in the hallways on the way to class, never knowing how they would inevitably be linked.

The arrest of an alleged serial killer always makes the news. Later that morning, the story moved on the National Associated Press Wire with the following headline:

ARREST MADE IN MURDER, MAY BE LINKED TO
OTHER MISSING WOMEN

The article reiterated the facts in the case, with the news that the alleged killer, Kendall L. Francois, had been arrested by police and was in custody. The case had gone national and would stay that way.

Bill Siegrist reported to work early the next morning. It was amazing how much more energy he had now that Francois was in custody. Then Mannain walked in. They had both had just a few hours of restless sleep.

Without saying a thing, the two cops walked up to each other and shook hands heartily. They smiled. That was something they hadn't done at work in a long time. There were tears in their eyes. They had shared a bond that few people would ever know.

They really did look like astronauts in their Tyvek coveralls and masks. There were over eleven crime specialists in all, led by Tommy Martin. They were following the advanced, standard operating procedure the state police used when processing a crime scene where bodies may be buried.

The eleven men and women lined up shoulder to shoulder outside the house. With Rosa supervising, they placed, in even rows, brown, sterile paper about four feet from the house and raked stuff onto it that had fallen onto the grass and weeds. No telling what they might get that could be of value later.

When that job was done, they moved, uniformly, away from the house. They examined the ground, putting evidence flags in the ground next to something that shouldn't, in the normal course of things, be there.

Inside the house, Martin led four other crime-scene specialists in processing the area in the attic and crawl space where the bodies had been found. Five hundred-watt halogen lights on slim poles were set up to provide illumination. The power supply was a motor home that stood outside, the crime specialists' home away from home.

Eight bodies in total had shown up inside the house, eight of nine missing women. Where was the ninth?

"We worked hard on the scene," Martin remembered. "We wanted to document everything."

To help with that, full videotape was taken of the interior and exterior, both before and after the search.

When the crime scene outside had been completely gone over, and nothing unusual had shown up pending laboratory analysis of some of the more difficult to identify detritus, they brought in ground-penetrating radar. Men carrying what looked like treasure-hunting radar scopes walked slowly over the ground, waiting for the machines' sirens to go off, which would signal that a body had been found.

The radar picked up any spatial disturbances belowground, that might indicate earth had been dug out, then the hole refilled, with a body or bodies in it. But despite this technology, the ninth body did not turn up.

The investigators next turned to the garage. Through checking records, it was discovered that the concrete floor of the rear garage was new, less than a year old. It could easily have been installed to hide bodies buried underneath by the killer in the house.

Jackhammers were brought in and the neighbors were treated to the racket. The concrete garage floor was completely drilled out. With that done, sequential trenches were dug into the underlying earth. Nothing was found save worms. No evidence of human remains.

Back up in the house, with the crime scene fully processed, Martin and Rosa were now ready to remove the bodies for autopsy and identification. This was a delicate part of the investigation, because there might be evidence under the bodies. Martin and Rosa had the most experience at spotting the unusual.

"When you remove a body," says Martin, "the first thing you do is open up the covering surrounding it, in this case, the bags, and take photos. I look closely around the bodies. If I see any plastic, I secure it in an evidence envelope and have it checked for prints later."

Two of the bodies in the crawl space had been placed one on top of the other. They were just a little bit buried.

"We excavate with whisk brooms and clay garden trowels, so no possible evidence can be damaged," Martin continued.

It was physically difficult work. Both men were six footers working in a crawl space that had a two-foot ceiling. One by one, the skeletons were removed, each placed onto a metal gurney, and a white sheet placed over them. Then the grisly remains were wheeled out in the warm autumn sunshine.

Everyone in the media, from Maine to California, had heard about the case. Flashes went off in the faces of the cops who wheeled the bodies to a waiting van. Harsh TV lights mounted on top of video cameras recorded the proceedings for the local evening news.

It would not be until the third day, September 5, that all the bodies were finally removed pending autopsy by Dr. Barbara Wolf, the state's forensic pathologist at her Albany office.

"After we got the bodies out, we asked, 'What else is there?' " says Martin.

What was left was the dirt in the crawl space that might contain evidence that could further tie Francois to the murders. Using five-gallon buckets, the earth was slowly emptied out, sifted, and marked from what part of the crawl space it came from. They followed the same procedure in the attic. Of the five women there in the trash bags, Martin noticed that one of the bodies had a little bit of skin on its fingertip. It was the only one.

Another body had two rings on one hand. They were removed and the ground underneath sifted for evidence. Eventually, when the two crime specialists finished at the Francois house, they headed up to state police headquarters in Albany.

The new state police headquarters was located off the New York State Thruway at exit 24, a little south of downtown Albany. It was the same place where Senior Investigator Jimmy Ayling worked.

The building itself was a low-lying, modernistic, drab-looking cube. On one side of it was an array of antenna and satellite uplink dishes, making it very clear that the building housed state-of-the-art communications systems. Curiously enough, it had not cost the taxpayers a cent.

"The new building was built with money confiscated from drug dealers and other lawbreakers," Ayling explained.

Those miscreants had kindly financed what on the inside was a surprisingly spacious place, done in white and pale gray, with an open conference center on the bottom floor behind glass doors. Ringed above it on the upper floors were balconies that led to roomy offices. Even the cubicles, where some of the crime specialists sat, looked spacious and neat.

The first floor was honeycombed with examination rooms, shiny and white, filled with all kinds of futuristic-looking scientific apparatus. Some of the rooms were furnished with antiseptic white walls and shiny metal examining tables. It was on these tables, surrounded by closets filled with medical supplies, that the remains of the eight bodies would be placed for further examination and autopsy.

Outside, on the rear loading dock, the ambulance containing the women's remains had just arrived from Poughkeepsie. As Ayling watched, the rear doors were thrown open, the covered bodies taken out on gurneys and rolled into two of the first-floor examination rooms. Dr. Barbara Wolf, assistant chief medical examiner, prepared to do the autopsies.

Using dental records, Wolfe identified a body almost immediately as that of Catina Newmaster. The local police and prosecutor were notified. Wasting no time, Dutchess County District Attorney William Grady filed charges against Kendall L. Francois: the murder in the second degree of Catina Newmaster.

Murder in the second degree is not a capital charge. Until Grady could prove premeditation, he couldn't file for murder one. But he was confident that, when all the facts came out, he would be able to upgrade the charge to murder one, which meant he could ask for the death penalty.

With the indictment handed down, the recriminations started, beginning at no less a conspicuous place than the front page of the *New York Times*. The headline on page one of the paper, September 4, 1998, read:

POLICE ARE CRITICIZED AS POUGHKEEPSIE
HOUSE YIELDS CORPSES

The article quoted Georgiana Johnson, who was present while the police processed the crime scene. Johnson "said that her daughter Debbie Annan had twice told the police that she barely escaped alive from an encounter with Mr. Francois, who had picked her up on the corner of Academy and Montgomery Streets, took her to his home for paid sex and tried to strangle her."

Speaking for her daughter, Johnson claimed that Annan "occasionally helped police in undercover drug operations" and "had given detectives Mr. Francois's name and address."

Johnson also said the cops ignored her. Annan, she said, was now free of her addiction to crack and was working "double shifts as a cashier at a convenience store" in Ocala, Florida.

Serial killers might not be the *Times'* cup of

tea, but there was no question it helped sell newspapers. The *Times,* though, seemed to drop the ball. No mention was made in the article of whether or not Annan had filed a complaint against Francois, without which the police were powerless to do anything. But not to be outdone by their tabloid rival the *Daily News,* which the previous day had a story on Francois with a headline that screamed SERIAL SLAYER EYED, the *Times* article continued with charges against the police.

The *Times* cited a story similar to Annan's that was told by a "one-time prostitute . . . interviewed on tape by Irene Cornell of WCBS Radio. The woman said that she told police that Mr. Francois had tried to strangle her in November 1996, a month after the first disappearance in the case. She remembered that during the assault Mr. Francois suddenly stopped himself from choking her and said, 'Oh my God, I almost did it again.' "

This was inconsistent with what all of the other women who had had close encounters had reported. Francois had mentioned nothing about this during his confession. It is highly doubtful that had he said such a thing, implicating himself in the murders, and police were aware he said it, that they wouldn't have followed it up instead of spending two frustrating years trying to put a case together against the psychopath.

What the radio report really implied was that because the victims were prostitutes, the cops didn't pursue the case as aggressively as they would have if the victims had been respectable civilians.

"All the complaints that came to us were handled in a proper manner and we have done everything we can to solve this crime," Siegrist said in the article. No less a participant than Patricia Barone, Gina Barone's mother, came to the defense of the police.

"They absolutely did their job. They picked up on it the day I reported her missing and took it from there," said Barone.

Barone maintained her calm.

"In my head, I'd come to terms with it," she explained. "I had a feeling she was gone all this time. I always felt when the good Lord thought I was ready to hear it, I'd hear it."

For his part, District Attorney Grady remained closemouthed. He had learned from a previous high-profile case to treat the press very gingerly. Grady declined to enumerate details of the task force's investigation, but he did admit that other women had come forward with stories of having rough sex with Francois.

"Just because incidents took place doesn't mean arrests can happen," he accurately pointed out. "You need probable cause, sufficient evidence," which the *Times* failed to inform its reading public.

The article concluded with a quote from Giovanna Vellone, seventeen, who attended Arlington Middle School at the time Francis was a hall monitor there.

"He gave out lots of detentions for everything," Vellone said, though what that had to do with Kendall Francois being a serial killer was unclear, not to mention confusing.

The recriminations continued, with speculation in the *Poughkeepsie Record* about why Francois had been able to get his school jobs despite his arrest and conviction on a sexual charge.

"A guy who had bodies in his house was working in their middle school," said Assemblyman John Guerin, a Republican conservative who served in the state legislature as a representative from Ulster County across the river. Guerin also felt that Democratic Assembly Leader Sheldon Silver should bear some of the blame for Francois's ability to commit his crimes while still an employee of the school district.

"For over twenty years, New York City schoolchildren have been protected by a law that requires criminal background checks on all school employees. Silver has not permitted that to become law for the rest of New York's schoolchildren," said Guerin.

Politicians like Guerin, and the pontificating TV reporters looked at the Francois case as one giant morality play. There had to be good and evil and most important, someone to blame for the killer's very existence and his ability to commit his crimes in secret.

That Kendall Francois was not only intelligent but also clever; that he was physically strong enough to subdue his victims without any outcry so that no one heard him as he killed; none of those things counted as much as laying blame. The "other guy's" shoulders were as good a place as any.

"If a school district had any reason to not believe someone, we would investigate their background. School districts take people at their word," said Education Department spokesman Bill Hirschen in the story.

Added Arlington School Superintendent Donald Rothman: "If there was a violation for solicitation, we would have fired him. I would have said, 'You're outta here.'"

No one bothered to mention that it's awfully hard to catch a guy like Francois, who acts as normal as the next guy and yet is practicing his serial-killing craft in the shadows. People needed good guys and bad guys, and even though the truth lay somewhere in between, that just wouldn't do.

The public expected all the principals in the case to be tied up with a neat bow and fitted into either one of those categories. The alternative was even worse: despite being suspected by the police, a serial killer was free to continue his killing without fear of punishment or reprisal. These kinds of opinions received as much ink as the reactions from the families of the deceased.

In the wake of the big man's arrest, nothing was more poignant than the printed comments from the grieving families. Marguerite Marsh recalled that in the fall of 1996, her daughter Catherine Marsh had wanted to come home. She figured she had her drug addiction beat.

"She was a very good student, basketball

player and a lovely little girl with everything going for her until that cocaine got her," said Marsh. "I want everyone to know the good side. She was a beautiful girl."

After years of being addicted to drugs, she had entered and was completing a rehabilitation program in Dutchess County. She called home to tell her mother, Marguerite, of her progress. Not only was she completing her rehab, she wanted to get custody again of her two children and maybe even get a college degree. But her mother wasn't so sure.

"I was afraid if she came up here, she was going to continue with her habit. But she kept calling and calling and finally I said, 'Okay, come.' That was the last I ever heard from her."

Heidi Cramer, the daughter of Sandra French, said, "I have mixed feelings. In a way, I hope they don't find her because then she could be still alive. But in a way, it would be closure and this whole thing has been horrible.

"As for Francois, I would like to put him in the electric chair. I think he should be put in the chair and let each of us have a turn at pulling that handle down. Let's do it over and over until he's dead."

Christopher Briggs, Catina Newmaster's boyfriend, recalled her as a mother of five who loved flowers and dreamed of the ocean.

"She wanted to straighten out her life and be with her kids. But Catina had a very bad drug problem. She cried on my shoulder about it a lot. People in Dutchess County have said the cops shouldn't have even bothered looking for these women, that it was just one less crackhead or prostitute on the street. But these people all had families, and they shouldn't be forgotten."

Perhaps it was Patricia Barone who had the best handle on the fallout from the murders. Barone, who had already been caring for her daughter's daughter at the time of the junior Barone's disappearance, said, "In the beginning, you know, it was 'Where's my mommy?' And I'd tell her, 'Your mommy doesn't feel well. Mommy went away for a while.' Then we'd say, 'We're looking for your mommy and can't find her.' Now it's going to be, 'Your mommy's not coming home.'"

The Francois family was heard from, too. While father, Nat, mother, Paulette, and sisters Raquelle and Kierstyn refused steadfastly to comment in the press, their cousin, MonRay Francois, took over as the unofficial family spokesman.

MonRay Francois did not go looking for the very public limelight that he had been thrust into. It fell to him because he was the only Francois with a listed phone number in the general area. Thus he was the one who received the anonymous calls.

"They say things like, 'I suggest you watch your back,'" Francois told the *Poughkeepsie Journal*. "I think they want to lash out. I'm sorry for their loss, but you can't pick your family members."

Despite no evidence to the contrary, he

seemed to be assuming that the threatening phone calls came from the families of his cousin's victims. Francois maintained that in the days after the bodies were discovered, he had been in contact with Kendall Francois's siblings, who said that they were paying more attention to their mother's health as she dealt with the shock.

"She's a beautiful person and a sweet lady," said MonRay Francois.

Francois revealed that the father, whom he called "Nat," was mild mannered, very quiet, but fun to be around, "a lot like Kendall."

That was a first in American criminal jurisprudence. No one had ever described a serial killer as fun to be around.

Reporters flocked to ask MonRay Francois about his cousin's early background. Francois thought there was nothing back there, in his past that could even remotely explain Kendall Francois's actions.

"I don't know what made him tick. We'll have to wait for the movie," he said.

In fact, MonRay Francois was a bit perturbed that reporters kept asking him questions, as though he were some sort of expert on his cousin, which clearly he was not.

"People expect me to answer questions, thinking everybody's so tight," he said. "I'm sure everybody has family members they just say, 'Hi, what's up?' and ' 'bye' to, without having deep personal conversations."

For MonRay, the whole experience was more than a bit confusing.

"I have so many questions and there's only four people who can answer them—the people that lived in that house. And some of the questions, I'm not really sure I want the answers. For all this stuff that happened, that's not the mild-mannered Kendall I know."

A mild-mannered Kendall Francois was not the man the Poughkeepsie street women were familiar with. It sounded as though MonRay Francois really didn't know his cousin very well. He also did not have an answer as to how the family lived with the stench of the rotting bodies except the one that Kendall had supplied— the odor came from a family of dead raccoons in the attic.

MonRay Francois claimed to know Catina Newmaster and Michelle Eason. How, he didn't say. He also suspected that Kendall might have known some of the women from high school. But that was all it was, a suspicion, with no basis in fact. As for the rest of the family, MonRay said that he went out dancing with the sisters Kierstyn and Raquelle. Kendall, however, was not one of his buddies.

Commenting on the women his cousin Kendall chose as victims, Francois continued, "No matter what their lifestyle was, I don't think they deserve that [being murdered]."

In between all the media coverage, Tommy Martin and the forensic crew continued in their work. On September 4, they positively identified Audrey Pugliese as one of the women they had taken from the attic. Identifying her through medical records, the cops also had her driver's license, which Kendall Francois had saved as a souvenir. It was pretty damning evidence.

Tommy Martin remembered something that would aid in the identification of the victims. Martin wanted to get a crack at the one body that had the peeling skin on its fingertip. He went up to Albany and found the body he was looking for on the cold autopsy table in the antiseptic examination room. Using forceps, scalpel and tweezers, Martin removed the skin that remained on the one corpse's pinky finger.

Once he had it, he placed it on a glass slide and lightly covered it with fingerprint ink. Then he pressed a second slide on top of the first, sandwiching the dyed skin in between. When placed under a microscope, what showed up on the skin were the ridge details of the victim's fingerprint. It was photographed using a digital camera.

If the victim was, as suspected, a prostitute, she should have a record. The photograph of the fingerprint was scanned into a computer, which then processed it through the state's fingerprint database of women suspected and convicted of crimes. Almost immediately, they got a hit.

The woman's name was Wendy Meyers. It would be the third victim identified. She had been the first to disappear. A thirty-year-old known prostitute and drug user, her favorite place to pick up johns had been Poughkeepsie's Main Street, not too far from Kendall Francois's home.

Notified of her death, Meyers's relatives remembered a bright, young girl who had become addicted to a substance as deadly as Francois's strong hands.

The attempts at identification of the other victims continued. While Wolf did her autopsies as best she could with what was left of the victims, Poughkeepsie detectives subpoenaed the medical and dental records of all the missing prostitutes. The medical records would be useful if any of the women had had broken bones that had been set.

A forensic dentist was called in to match the dental records to the teeth in the bodies. Because teeth survive bodily decomposition, they present the best chance for a matching identification.

September 5, 1998

Back in Poughkeepsie, the police continued their search of the Francois home. The residents on Fulton Avenue began to adjust to the fact that they had had a serial killer in their midst and never knew about it. When reporters did man-on-the-street interviews with them and the question was inevitably asked, "Did you suspect anything," the answer was always the same.

No one had seen anything suspicious, like Francois strangling girls in his car in the backyard in broad daylight, or escorting some of the live ones into his house, also in broad daylight, never to return. It was just that strange smell.

As the investigation progressed into the next week, the Francois home became a tourist attraction. Tourists had the luxury of being able to look at the home of a killer and not think anything good about him. They had the luxury of looking at the true face of evil, which, of course, wasn't very dramatic.

The fact was, most homicides involved people who knew each other. They were human beings who made mistakes. They might be vile humans, but they were human nevertheless. A serial killer was different. His mere kill total meant he could be looked at without extenuating circumstances.

To answer the question—What does the face of evil look like?—one merely had to look at the banal visage of Kendall Francois. Want to know what a murder house looks like? Easy. Come to Fulton Avenue in Poughkeepsie. And that's exactly what people did.

It became a big carnival. People from the city and town, from surrounding towns, from all over three counties, came to Fulton Avenue to look at the home of a serial killer. The media christened it "Poughkeepsie's House of Horrors."

People gathered on the sidewalk in front of the house and watched the Tyvek-clad technicians ply their trade. They saw the crime-scene specialists take hundreds and hundreds of bags of evidence out of the house. They gaped at the news vans that staked the place out as though they still expected something dramatic to come from the investigation.

The great film director Billy Wilder, who died in 2002, had once directed a film called *The Big Carnival*, which was about a man trapped in a mine cave-in, the reporter who secretly hampers rescue efforts to "hype" the story, and the carnival that forms outside the cave as rescue workers try to get him out. It was a cynical work, even for the usually cynical Wilder. But if hot dog stands and rides had been added to the carnival outside the Francois home, life would have definitely been doing a perfect imitation of art.

One neighbor, Gary Eckstein, had gotten so sick and tired of the spectacle and the roadblocks on Fulton Avenue that he had to negotiate every day since the discovery, and the smell that still emanated from the house, that he had moved out until the whole thing was over.

"I couldn't understand why people stood out there for hours and just stared. They were there with their kids in strollers," said Eckstein in a local paper.

It was the same kind of mentality that makes some drivers slow down when they approach an accident on the other side of the road. There's a vicarious thrill in seeing human tragedy that isn't part of you and yours. Sometimes, people who didn't even know them, have a need to recognize the dead.

The tree on Eckstein's property closest to the street had become a shrine to the dead women.

It was filled with cards, ribbons, roses and flowers placed there to honor the victims.

"The first day there was just a bouquet of roses in front of the tree. The next day it was covered with the stuff," Eckstein recalled.

But his real concern was that when the police finally completed their investigation and left, what would happen then? Who would be there to keep the morbid and the curious out of his yard and the yards of other houses that afforded a bird's-eye view of the lair of the serial killer?

For the Francois family, who were also displaced, the questions were much more far reaching.

What do you do when your son/brother is a suspected serial killer? How do you feel, knowing, knowing that your flesh and blood is suspected of being a modern-day Jack the Ripper? Does it send shivers up your spine, or do you just face it with the inevitability of having known what was really going on and turning, for your own reasons, a blind eye to it?

No one would ever know. The Francois family got a lawyer, Marco Caviglia, to speak for them. Aside from expressing the family's sympathy to the victims and their families, he said nothing about the crimes, their son and brother, nothing that would shed any light on the reasons for such wholesale murder.

Kendall Francois's parents and sister would not speculate publicly about why their son and brother was a serial killer.

PART THREE
A Matter of
Life or Death

Fourteen

The tortoise had won the race. The tortoise in this case was the City of Poughkeepsie Police Department. The hare was Kendall Francois. For two years, the hare had led until finally the tortoise caught up.

After two years of work, Bill Siegrist and Skip Mannain and their ally Jimmy Ayling at the state police had finished their active involvement in the case. They would come in and out as the following weeks and months would lead to what for all was an unknown outcome.

Would Francois be convicted of murder one and sentenced to death? Or, would he be convicted of or plead to a lesser charge, thereby avoiding death? It could all be up to Bill Grady. It was Grady who now took center stage in the still unfolding drama of the serial killer's life.

William "Bill" Vincent Grady was a local. Fifty-six years old, he had been born in Beacon, just a few miles south of Poughkeepsie. He had grown up in Dutchess County. It was his luck to be born into a prominent family.

Grady's father, Vincent, had been the county's district attorney in the 1940's. Like many politicians who don the district attorney's suit, he wished for higher office and got it. Eventually, Dutchess County District Attorney Vincent Grady became Justice Grady of the New York State Supreme Court.

In most states, the supreme court is the highest court in the state, but not in cockeyed New York. The Empire State reserve that honor for the court of appeals. No, Vincent Grady spent his time as a judge presiding over the matters the supreme court had the jurisdiction of—trials for murder, robbery, kidnapping and other felonies.

Bill Grady aspired to the bar and to follow in his father's footsteps. Fate had other plans. During the height of the Vietnam War in the tumultuous 1960's, Bill Grady served his country as a captain in an armored unit in the most contentious war in United States history. Vietnam is a small country on an Asian continent far away from his bucolic home in Dutchess County. In combat, he acquitted himself admirably: he won the Bronze Star for bravery under fire.

Returning home, he attended and graduated from New York Law School. In 1971, he went to Poughkeepsie, the county seat, and became an assistant district attorney. In the courtroom or out, Grady did not cut a dashing figure. He was slight of build and height, bespectacled,

with a tight, bland face, hardly the image con-
jured up of "the fighting DA" of fiction and
film. Plus, the county's newest ADA had neither
the oratory nor charisma of the state's most famous prosecutor, Thomas E. Dewey, who put
Lucky Luciano away and later used that as a
platform to run for president.

Grady also did not have the brilliant legal
mind of some in his profession. Instead, Bill
Grady's technique was slow and steady. Not too
much flash and dash, but he got the job done.
After working in the district attorney's office as
an assistant prosecutor for a couple of years,
he was promoted to chief assistant prosecutor.

The politics in Dutchess County are from the
old school. The dominating Republican political
machine controls political patronage. That, combined with blatant nepotism, is how the county
runs to this day. It functions within a system that
especially abhors outsiders' criticisms. Running
on the Republican ticket, Bill Grady lost his first
bid to become district attorney in 1975. Never
one to give up, he ran again in 1985.

Grady was a man of the people, a guy like
any other on the street. Like the average citizen, he was concerned about the high rate of
crime and the cost to the county's families and
resources. His rhetoric about crime and drugs
and their insidious effect on the county reso-
nated with voters.

Bill Grady won election to the office his father had once occupied. Since then, most observers have felt that Grady did his job and did
it well; the voters liked him and the Republican

political machine in the county was happy with his performance.

By 1988, Grady had been a prosecutor for almost twenty years. Killers, thieves, con men, robbers, rapists, he had prosecuted them all. He was experienced and professional. His reputation inside the county was established. Outside the county, few, except political insiders, knew who he was. That was fine; he did his job.

And then along came Tawana Brawley.

It happened in the fall of 1988. A fifteen-year-old girl named Tawana Brawley was discovered in a green plastic garbage bag on the site of an apartment complex in Wappinger Falls, the city directly south of Poughkeepsie. The venue was still Dutchess County. That meant that Grady as the DA directed all investigations.

Sheriff's deputies arrived and took in the scene. The girl, who appeared unconscious, had no obvious injuries. There was no blood, no bruising, nothing. Upon further physical examination, they discovered that "KKK" had been written across the top of the girl's chest. On her stomach, someone had written the word "Nigger." Feces were smeared on her arms and legs and it was the feces that provided the "ink" for the aforementioned epithets.

It was, to put it mildly, perplexing. What had happened? Had she been raped and then smeared with excrement by racists? The girl wouldn't say. She kept her eyes closed. They tried talking to her. Except for a fluttering of her eyelids, there was no response. The cops called an ambulance and the girl was whisked to nearby St. Francois Hospital, where she was examined.

There was no sign of rape. The girl appeared physically fine, but she wouldn't or couldn't talk. The ID in her wallet gave them her name. Her mother, Glenda Brawley, was called and she came to the hospital.

Tawana Brawley's method of communication consisted of nods and shakes of her head, shrugging shoulders and scrawling in the cop's notebook. After a few hours of talking to her like this, Brawley charged in grunts, groans and pictures that it was a group of white men, including at least one white cop, who had raped the girl over a period of four days. Her family brought in Alton H. Maddox, Jr., a black lawyer who specialized in civil rights cases to represent her. Brawley's legal team would later include another black lawyer familiar with civil rights cases, C. Vernon Mason. The Reverend Al Sharpton came on board as the third "family adviser."

Primarily an administrator, Grady initially assigned the case to two of his assistant district attorneys, including Marjorie Smith, the same Marjorie Smith who would later take Kendall Francois's statement. As the Brawley family advisers and the Brawley family made claims of racial bias in the investigation, as well as the crime, Grady got actively involved.

In an effort to ferret out the truth, Grady and a black assistant personally went to the Brawleys' apartment in Wappinger Falls. He practically begged Glenda Brawley to allow the teenager and her family to cooperate in the investigation.

Glenda Brawley was uncooperative and non-committal. Brawley's stepfather, Ralph King, broke up the meeting. He burst in the door, shouting obscenities highlighted by, "What the fuck is going on here?"

The prosecutors' jaws dropped. After some more verbal haranguing, they left. Meanwhile, the media had taken hold of the story. Well into 1989, the media hung on every word from the Brawley family and their advisers. Bowing to their pressure, Governor Mario Cuomo appointed Attorney General Bob Abrams as special prosecutor. Grady was effectively out of it.

After almost a yearlong investigation, on October 6, 1988, a grand jury Abrams had called issued a 170-page report. It consisted of 6,000 pages of testimony from 108 witnesses and 250 exhibits. The report concluded:

> Based upon all the evidence that has been presented to the grand jury, we concluded that Tawana Brawley was not the victim of a forcible sexual assault by multiple assailants over a four-day period. There is no evidence that any sexual assault occurred. The grand jury further concludes there is nothing in regard to Tawana Brawley's appearance on November 28 [the day she was found in the garbage bag] that is inconsistent with this condition having been self-inflicted.

In other words, the whole thing was a hoax. Brawley had manufactured the whole thing.

Why, was open to conjecture. Regardless of the reason, for Grady, the conclusion could not come soon enough.

It had been a bad experience for the DA, not one he wanted to repeat. Despite the subsequent discrediting of Tawana Brawley's story, Grady's office had seemed incompetent in handling the case, and the press had gone along with the view.

Since 1988, Grady had run and been reelected twice. There had been nothing that even came close to the attention he and his office received in the Tawana Brawley affair. His next reelection bid was in 1999. His constituents would be watching closely to see how he handled the prosecution of Kendall Francois.

There was never any question that Grady would seek the death penalty against the alleged serial killer. Ironically, a recently introduced death penalty law was so unclear in the way it was written that, even if Grady got a conviction, there was no guarantee Francois would be executed for his crimes. In a sense, the very nature of his crimes might guarantee him immunity.

On March 7, 1995, Governor George E. Pataki had signed a bill reinstating the death penalty in New York. After more than thirty years without it, New York, with its infamous electric chair at Sing Sing Prison, had the death penalty once again.

Both houses of the New York State legislature, the senate, and the assembly had previously passed the bill, by votes of thirty-eight to nine-teen, and ninety-four to fifty-two, respectively. There had been eighteen previous attempts by the senate and assembly to reintroduce the death penalty since 1977, but all the previous bills had been vetoed by former Democratic governors Cary and Cuomo. Those men believed that the death penalty was not only inhuman, but it was not a deterrent to capital crime.

In contrast, Governor Pataki, a Republican, had run on a platform that made the reinstatement of the death penalty the centerpiece of his future administration. His 1994 election as governor had moved the issue forward and guaranteed that he would sign the legislation. Upon his ascendancy, the death penalty bill had been the first major piece of legislation to be signed into law.

In reaction to the signing of the death penalty bill, former Governor Cuomo stated: "This is a step back in what should be a march constantly toward a higher level of civility and intelligence. The argument that the death penalty will deter and reduce crimes has been abandoned almost everywhere."

The way the legislators had written the statute, the new law allowed for death sentences to be imposed for approximately ten offenses. They included the following: intentional murder committed during the course of a rape, robbery or kidnapping; contract killings; the murder of prison wardens, police officers or other law enforcement officials; and murder involving torture. The law excluded those under eighteen years of age at the time of the offense, pregnant women and the mentally retarded from execution. The determination of mental retardation would be made by the trial court.

Under the death penalty statute, capital murder trials would have two phases. The first phase would determine the guilt or innocence of the defendant. Upon conviction of first-degree murder, the court would hold a second hearing known as the penalty phase. The penalty phase would determine whether a sentence of death or life imprisonment without the possibility of parole was to be imposed.

The decision on sentencing rested with the original trial jury that would be reimpaneled during the sentencing phase. The jury would be required to determine whether the mitigating facts pertaining to the defendant and the crime outweighed the aggravating factors. Mitigating factors included the defendant's lack of prior criminal record; whether the defendant suffered from mental retardation or impaired mental capacity at the time of the crime; and that the defendant was under duress or the domination of another person at the time of the offense. Aggravating factors included previous convictions for violent offenses, or that the crime was considered an act of terrorism.

A unanimous decision by the jury was required for either of the available sentences. In the event of the jury being unable to reach a unanimous decision, the defendant would be sentenced to life imprisonment with a minimum term of twenty years.

Detailed research, both in the United States and other countries, has produced no evidence that the death penalty deters crime more effectively than any other punishment. In many nondeath-penalty countries, the homicide rate has decreased after the abolition of capital punishment. For example, in Canada the death penalty was abolished in 1976. From the date of its abolition until the end of 1993, the rate of homicides per 100,000 population has dropped by twenty-seven percent.

Figures from other countries made no difference, though. Governor Pataki cited prevention of violent crime as his major justification for reintroducing capital punishment. He knew that if the public did not want its revenge, the death penalty would not exist.

No politician in his right mind who expected to be reelected in a conservative county, which Grady served in, could advocate against the death penalty, let alone not impose it in the worst case of serial murder in New York State history. Electrocution had once been the method of execution. The new law made execution more humane. The killer convicted of murder one would see his life ended by lethal injection. Old Sparky at Sing Sing would remain inactive.

An act was also passed making a provision of eleven million dollars, "or so much thereof as may be necessary," to cover the increased prosecution and defense costs involved in administering death penalty laws. This included the establishment of the Capital Defender Office, a state body charged with defending those

who were being prosecuted under the new
death penalty statute.

At the bill-signing ceremony in 1995, Pataki
used two pens that had previously belonged to
murdered police officers. The relatives of homicide victims surrounded him. Governor Pataki
was quoted as stating, "Justice will now be
served. . . . It is a solemn moment because this
is something aimed at preventing tragedy, and
we've seen too many tragedies in the past."

Solemn moment or not, Pataki's death penalty bill was terribly flawed. Serial killing did
not necessarily warrant the death penalty and
in the case of Kendall Francois, even less so.

Francois could claim that he had strangled
the women during a business transaction—sex
for money, usually known as prostitution. That
certainly did not qualify as rape under the law,
which meant Francois had not intentionally
killed while committing another felony.

Nor had he planned the killings. They seemed
to happen at the moment. Only if a murder was
planned in advance could the prosecution jus-
tify a capital murder one charge.

As for the serial aspect of the crimes, the statute says that murder punishable by death falls
under the death penalty law if "the defendant
intentionally caused the death of two or
more . . . persons within the state in separate
criminal transactions within a period of twenty-
four hours when committed in a similar fashion
or pursuant to a common scheme or plan."

In other words, the statute defined serial killing as two or more murders committed within

the state, on separate occasions, "within a period of twenty-four hours." Under the state's own definition of serial killing, Kendall Francois did not fall into that category.

If Francois opted for diminished capacity, commonly known as the insanity defense, Grady would have to prove that Francois was sane at the time of the crimes. That might be difficult. What sane man commits serial murder?

Francois's very crimes might be the actual defense that kept him from being strapped to a gurney and having poison injected into his blood. It was like he had a "get out of death free" card. And, if the jury didn't vote for death, what then? It was entirely possible that the worst he could be sentenced to was life behind bars without parole. But who knew if that really meant life?

Somewhere along the line, some reformers would change the law. Lifers like Francois could be given paroles. Even Nathan Leopold, who, along with his friend Richard Loeb, was convicted of the most famous thrill killing in United States history and received a life sentence in the 1920's, was later given parole during the 1950's.

Life didn't necessarily mean life. But sentencing was a long way off. In order to prosecute an individual successfully, the state needs to know his or her official background. It helps in establishing a time line, especially in cases of serial killing. Plus there might actually be something in the individual's background that could further assist the state in its prosecution.

Fifteen

Siegrist and company zeroed in on Kendall Francois's military service. Could he have committed serial murder while he was in the army stationed in Hawaii? A check of the records showed that there was, indeed, a serial killer operating in Hawaii while Francois was stationed there. The Poughkeepsie Police Department immediately contacted the Honolulu Police Department.

"We had focused on a suspect [who wasn't Francois] but there wasn't enough to bring him to trial," said Honolulu Police Lieutenant Allan Napoleon. Napoleon headed up the city's homicide squad.

Napoleon pointed out that unlike the Poughkeepsie case, in Hawaii the victims were all blondes and their bodies dumped near the ocean and streams. Since the victims' descriptions didn't match Poughkeepsie's, the connection was discounted.

Plus, Napoleon said, when their suspect left the area, "It [the killings] stopped."

That seemed to pretty much rule out Francois. The police did not follow up on Francois's time during basic training at Fort Sill, in Oklahoma, to see if there were any unsolved murders there. Reading about all this in the newspapers, which covered every detail of the official investigation, the Francois family couldn't help but be interested, but not interested enough to make any public comment. Speaking for them, their lawyer, Marco Caviglia, told how the Francoises were forced to leave their daughter's apartment, where they'd been staying since the night of their dispossession.

"The Francois family is still homeless," attorney Caviglia told the media. "Because of the allegations of unkemptness at the former family residence . . . they have been denied the right to rent."

The Francoises had no choice but to rent, since their house was literally still in police custody. It was doubtful, too, if they would go back there to live; it wouldn't be safe. The public perception was that there were too many people Francois had allegedly harmed who would, in turn, want revenge.

Their only choice was to rent until the house was released, at which point they could try to sell it. Unfortunately for them, state law requires full disclosure about a house's sordid history, not that any was really needed in this case since it got so much media coverage. That kind of unwarranted attention could do nothing but lower the sale price.

While the Francoises continued to contemplate their uncertain future, Grady convened a grand jury to formally charge Kendall Francois. It was the first step on a path that Grady hoped would eventually lead Kendall Francois into the death chamber.

Unlike in the Brawley case, this time Grady controlled the story. Not one word about the police investigation, city, county or state, got out without his prior okay. Police officers were instructed not to talk to the press unless they checked with his office first. But despite his attention to detail, Grady found himself once again in over his head. He made the wrong decision.

The first thing the press latched on to was the seeming incompetence of the police in tracking the serial killer down. Charge after charge appeared in the press that the cops had blown it. The September 3 *New York Times* article was the best example of the popular perception that the cops had been apathetic toward the victims.

The perception was that the cops thought the women were just worthless prostitutes. Feeling that way, they did not devote their full resources to bringing the killer to ground. As a result, he continued to kill with seeming impunity because of the way he picked his victims: the flotsam of society that no one, including the public, really cared about.

To Siegrist, the truth was it had not made any difference. They had pursued the killer through two years and eight changes of season. It made no difference to them who the victims were; the public could believe what it wanted. They had not given up and through careful, plodding police work, they had gotten him.

That wasn't enough.

Now that the savagery of Kendall Francois had been exposed to the light, someone needed to shoulder the blame for his reign of terror. Had the politicians given law enforcement more support to begin with, had given them more financial resources to tackle the case, maybe, maybe Francois would have been brought in sooner.

No matter.

Someone needed to take the blame. As usual, the police were the best candidates. Also working against further disclosure in the case were the vagaries of New York State law.

In terms of the police investigation, normally after a forensics examination of the crime scene, detectives are dispatched to pound the pavement in search of evidence and to do interviews with people who can provide leads to the killer's identity. But in the Francois case, it was all backward. There was no crime scene to investigate.

By the time Francois confessed, any real evidence of the murders in his bedroom, aside from a few trinkets that belonged to the victims, was gone. Should he decide to recant his confession and say he gave it under duress, a good lawyer could plant reasonable doubt in a jury's mind that he had gotten those things voluntarily from the victims.

Grady's quest to see Francois hang would not be an easy one. He would have court-appointed adversaries up to the challenge of saving the serial killer's life.

* * *

Albany

Dr. Barbara Wolf and her forensic team continued to examine the bodies of the victims.

None of the victims had neck tissue with fingermarks on it because there was no skin, just necrotic tissue. Because of this kind of decomposition, the state police medical examiner and her team were unfortunately unable to gather much evidence from the bodies regarding cause of death. They were, however, able to ascertain through breaks in the victims' hyoid bones that they had been strangled.

Identifying the victims was much easier. Medical and dental records were compared. One by one, over the next few days, the victims were identified. The last to be identified was Kathleen Hurley on September 8.

"She left early one afternoon and never came back to her apartment," her brother Jim DeSalvo said to the press.

DeSalvo revealed that his sister had become "heavily involved with drugs, especially crack, after their mother died." Most tellingly, DeSalvo was not surprised that his "sister hung around people like Francois prior to her death."

September 10, 1998

The Francois family was distraught. They just could not believe what had happened to Kendall and how they themselves had been dispossessed. That was the substance of the statement their attorney, Marco Caviglia, delivered to the press.

"We find ourselves plagued by unimaginable circumstance," said the statement. "Our youngest son is suspected of committing grave offenses from which his life hangs in the balance. We have virtually lost everything, been dispossessed of our home and cast into the street."

Better than cast into the attic or crawl space.

"We are without access to funds, lodging, food or valuable personal papers."

As part of the investigation, the police had seized all their personal papers and looked into their bank accounts. It was actually standard operating procedure. Police always look for a link between the victim and murderer, such as money or letters changing hands. The more that link can be shown, the easier it is to convict.

"The family requests that under these extraordinary circumstances, the public and media respect the only two items we have now, our privacy and personal rights."

September 15, 1998

New York is not Texas. The Lone Star State has been accused of providing inadequate legal representation in capital murder cases. That's one reason why Texas has the highest rate of executions in this country—some of the public

defenders that represent indigent murderers
are not up to the task.

New York is different.

When Governor Pataki reinstated the death
penalty, there was no one then practicing in
the state that had actually worked a death penalty case. The last murder that involved a sentence of death was back in the 1960's.

New York's legislators, in passing the governor's death penalty law, realized they had to
level the playing field. State-sanctioned revenge
was nothing to trifle with. So as part of the 1995
death penalty statute, the Capital Defender Office (CDO) was created with public funding.

The CDO was given the mandate to provide
"legal, investigative and expert witness services
to indigent defendants who are charged, or
could potentially be charged, with first-degree
murder." It didn't need a legal expert to figure
out that Kendall Francois could potentially be
charged with capital murder. If he wasn't, that
would have been a surprise.

One of the first things that happened after
he was taken into custody was a call going out
to the Capital Defender Office in Albany. Randolph Treece, a lawyer with the office, was appointed as Francois's counsel. The murderer
would also have the assistance, as circumstances
required, of any resources the office had to offer.

And who was paying for all of this? Why, the
good people of New York State. Every year, almost fifteen million dollars of tax money was
allocated by the state legislature to fund the

activities of the Capital Defender Office, this after the executive branch of the state government requested the actual appropriation. Therein lay the irony.

The office of the governor headed up the executive branch. While the governor advocated the death penalty, he also had to agree, as part of the death penalty law, to allocate significant monies to the death penalty opponents that occupied the Capital Defender Office.

Kendall Francois would be convicted of murder. That was practically a certainty. The only real defense he had was diminished capacity and that was almost impossible to prove. As in many cases involving the death penalty, the real drama was not over conviction, but conviction on what charge?

If it were murder one with life imprisonment, that would be a significant victory for the CDO. If the conviction also included death as the penalty, not only would that be a legal defeat, a man would lose his life. Despite his crimes, the death penalty opponents in the CDO thought it wrong to institute state-sanctioned death and revenge.

The CDO's first challenge was curtailing the adverse publicity. Newspapers had named Francois the "Poughkeepsie Serial Killer." He was being compared to the worst serial killers of all time. That had to stop because of the jury pool.

Everyone reading an article about him, seeing a news report about him, was a potential juror. They would form an opinion. Invariably, it would be negative. At trial, during the penalty phase, that negativity could mean a vote for death. The idea for the CDO was not to present a favorable portrait of the murderer. In this case, there really was none, but they could work to at least control the hemorrhaging.

In court papers submitted to Thomas Dolan, the presiding judge assigned to the Francois case, Treece claimed that Grady had "trampled" on his client's right to a fair trial by sharing information on the case with the press. What Treece objected to specifically was a statement Grady made in which he said that Francois had talked with police about the bodies inside his house. Treece wanted to have the court record of Francois's statements to police sealed from the public.

Responding to Treece's entreaty that Francois was being denied a fair trial, Chief Assistant District Attorney William O'Neill said Grady had the right and the obligation as an elected official to share certain facts about the case with the public.

"The Capital Defender's Office properly indicates that as officers of the court, attorneys share a legal and ethical responsibility to ensure the right to a fair trial," said O'Neill in papers submitted to Dolan. "Yet [the Capital Defender] ignores the duties and responsibilities that an elected official has in assuring the public that the investigation of criminal cases will not be conducted under a shroud of secrecy."

O'Neill was trying to tell the court that the DA was playing fair, by the rules, and simply informing his public what was what. Treece then asked Judge Thomas Dolan for a court order allowing his own forensic experts to perform their own autopsies on the bodies. While some of the families publicly groused that they couldn't bury their dead, Treece's motion was well intentioned.

A spokeswoman for the state's Capital Defender Office, said, "It's not unusual for the defense to have access to the autopsies when they're being performed. . . . That didn't happen here."

Treece publicly stated his sympathy for the families, but he still had a job to do.

"I think people assume that the district attorney's office is going to share with us what they ascertain from their autopsy," he said. "We need to know some vital information that would verify or differ from what they've found."

Of course, during discovery, the phase of trial where each side shares the evidence they plan to present to the jury, the DA is supposed to follow through on this legal obligation. While Grady played by the rules, there were other DAs in other localities who didn't.

Using some of the more than fourteen million dollars the governor and legislature had allocated to the CDO, Treece brought in a pathologist and an anthropologist. Both forensic experts, it was their job to assist in gathering evidence that might be helpful to the defense.

Like some of the other victims' relatives, Patricia Barone had already started making funeral plans. She had to stop until the defense experts finished with the bodies.

"If you bang your head against the wall," she said to the papers, "all you do is make yourself frustrated. I've waited a long time for my Gina."

The French family had planned on burying Sandra sooner rather than later. Even before her body was released, hers was the first obituary to appear in the *Poughkeepsie Journal* with a dateline of September 15.

"Sandra Jean French, 51, a lifelong resident of Dover Plains, was pronounced dead September 2 in Poughkeepsie."

The obituary did not list cause or method of death. No mention was made of Kendall Francois. Her family had arranged for calling hours at the Hufcut Funeral Home in Dover Plains. Because of the delay, the obituary concluded, "Burial will be private at the convenience of the family."

It actually didn't take long. Within days, the defense had finished with the remains. One by one, they were released to Dutchess County Medical Examiner Joseph Ross, who contacted the families to claim them. The women in death had told them all they could. It was time to allow them their final rest. The next three obituaries appeared on September 18 in the *Poughkeepsie Journal.*

"Gina Marie Barone, 29, a longtime Poughkeepsie resident, was found dead September 3 in Poughkeepsie."

"Wendy Meyers, 30, a 10-year Dutchess

County resident who had been missing since October 26, 1996, was found dead Feb. 2 [sic] in Poughkeepsie. She was a homemaker."

Describing Meyers as a homemaker might have been bending political correctness a little too much. She had a misdemeanor prostitution conviction on her record.

"Mary E. Healey Giaccone, 31, was found dead September 2 in Poughkeepsie. A nurse's aid at Fishkill Health Center in Beacon, she was a parishioner of St. Joachim's Church in Beacon."

That was news. Giaccone had held a regular job. The health center she worked at in Beacon, though, refused to comment on how she did and why she left. That wasn't surprising.

Those who knew the women were being sought out by the media. Anxious for a quote or sound bite, they'd take anyone who knew the women. Most, though, refused comment. They didn't want to be associated with a prostitute who had been killed by a serial killer. That they had an opportunity to humanize the women in the press, a press that regularly referred to their profession in a thinly veiled derogatory way, escaped them.

Its parishioners regularly called St. Joachim Church "St. Joey's." Located on Leonard Street in Beacon, it was a simple stone church that looked like it belonged in the quaint nineteenth century, not the bustling twentieth.

Inside, it was ornate and simple at the same

time, the wooden benches long since smoothed out by generations and generations of seated parishioners. In the back was the small font of holy water, and on the side were the votive candles lit by parishioners praying for something to happen in their lives that they wanted very much.

Mary Healey Giaccone, that bright-eyed teenager who had somehow gone down the wrong road, was a regular in this place. She could find the peace and serenity at St. Joey's that no other place on earth afforded her.

By ten A.M., the church was filled to capacity with relatives and friends of Healey Giaccone. The priest conducting the service celebrated a Mass of Christian Burial. Then it was time for one last ride. The pallbearers lifted and shouldered the casket, walking solemnly out the front doors into the light. They loaded the casket into the waiting hearse.

The funeral cortege crawled up Leonard Street to the Forestal School. It passed the Central Hudson substation and made a right onto Stone Street. Suddenly, there was a rushing stream on the left, achingly beautiful in the autumn sun. Then at the corner, a left at the new guardrails and up a ways to St. Joey's Cemetery.

The church's private cemetery is on a hill, with one of the Catskills peaks looming above it in the distance. It is a small cemetery, with veterans having special plaques on their stones singling them out for their service. The rest of the graves are nondescript. As Healey Giaccone's casket was being lowered into the ground, mourners cried and shuffled their feet in the awkward posture of the grieving. Then, after a while, they descended the hill to the waiting automobiles.

Mary Healey Giaccone was in her grave. It was a place that more and more in the community wanted to see Kendall Francois—six feet under.

September 29, 1998

"Let's close it down," Tommy Martin said.

Kevin Rosa nodded.

It was over. After twenty-seven long days of digging, sifting, prodding, poking, searching, the police were satisfied they had gotten all they could out of the crime scene at the Francois home.

Martin and Rosa removed the crime-scene tape that they had originally strung up almost a month before. They tossed it into the van and got ready to go. Martin took one long, last look up at the house.

We did a good job, he thought, *a good job.*

There was, however, one woman they did not find in the house. Michelle Eason was still missing. Reporters had tracked down Michelle Eason's brother Jerry Eason and he had commented on his sister's disappearance.

"She called me and we had a long talk," before she disappeared, said Eason. "When she called me again, she said she'd gotten herself together. She sounded much better. I could hear that in her voice. But that was that."

Francois had never mentioned Eason as one of the women he had killed. The cops still suspected he had done it. Without a body, or a burial location, there wasn't much they could do except keep the case active in their files. Homicides stay active indefinitely, until the case is closed. Unlike other crimes, there is no statute of limitation on homicides.

Martin closed the door to their van.

"We got another call," said Rosa, and he drove off to the next crime scene they had been called in to process.

September 30, 1998

Her journey to Poughkeepsie and sobriety unsuccessful, Catherine Marsh finally came home.

Forty people who had known Marsh gathered at the Boger House on North Hamilton Street in Rensselaer. The place had been decorated with dozens of photographs showing Marsh in better times, playing basketball and on family trips.

"Catherine Marsh: I am a woman of worth and integrity," the gathering was called. It was an opportunity for closure and good-byes. Many had come.

Cathy's mother, Marguerite, was there. So were her friends from the residential drug and alcohol facility that she had been staying at before her murder. Skip Mannain had also come to read her diary to all those assembled who were paying their respects.

Her diary mentioned many of the same people who were there for the gathering. Mannain said that in certain places in that book, she had written of her disappointment in failing her family and friends. She even chastised herself for missing a recovery meeting.

At the end of the service, Cathy Marsh's friends sang a lullaby they had written especially for her. In coming days, there would be more burials, more tears, more heartache.

October 13, 1998

Bill Grady moved forward with his case. He impaneled a grand jury to bring down indictments against Francois. Without much prodding, they did exactly that.

The grand jury handed down eight murder-one indictments, accusing Kendall L. Francois of intentionally strangling eight women. The law also allowed eight separate counts of second-degree murder. Almost as an afterthought, he was also charged with second-degree attempted assault for trying to strangle Diane Franco.

Grady's next decision was whether or not to seek the death penalty. By law, the district attorney has 120 days from the date of arraignment to make that decision. Grady anticipated a decision by January. First, though, was the formal arraignment.

October 14, 1998

The State Supreme Court was in an old building on Church Street, across the street from the Bardovan Theater where the Paper Bag Players were performing for the area's children. Inside, on the third floor of the building was Judge Dolan's courtroom. It was old-fashioned, the type seen in old Hollywood movies.

The place was paneled in burnished oak and mahogany, spacious with three sections for observers. There was the slatted wooden rail at the front separating the observers' section from the well of the courtroom where the court officers sat. On the left, looking toward the front, sat the DA; on the right sat counsel for the defense and the defendant.

Directly in front of them was the raised platform on which the court clerk and stenographer sat. Right above, high off the ground was the judge's bench, looking high and mighty in the morning sunshine streaming in from the floor-to-ceiling windows at the far side of the courtroom.

Never before had an entire section of a courtroom been taken up with the relatives of the victims. Most homicide cases involved one person. This one had eight—eight known. It was filled to capacity with the friends and relatives of Kathleen Hurley, Gina Barone, Cathy

Marsh, Mary Giaccone, Catina Newmaster, Wendy Meyers, Audrey Pugliese and Dover Plains' own Sandra French. Mothers, daughters, cousins, uncles, they were all there to see that justice was done.

A hushed courtroom suddenly erupted. There was electricity in the air as the door to the right of the bench opened. The man who had prompted that day's proceeding began to shuffle in. Kendall Francois had to shuffle because he was shackled from hand to ankle. The people watched anxiously as the man they thought of as a monster entered the court and took his place by his attorney, Randolph Treece's, side.

For a man facing death, Francois looked well fed and cared for, clean and satisfied. He wore an orange prison jumpsuit. Kendall Francois had been in jail over a month and the county was treating him well, almost like a prize goose being fattened up for the slaughter.

"Murderer!" one of the relatives shouted.

"Animal," chimed in another.

A few moments later, the judge walked in, his black robes flowing around him. Dolan mounted the bench and took his seat. The court clerk called the court to order.

"Proceed," said Judge Dolan to his clerk.

It was a formal arraignment, a proceeding where the exact charges against the defendant were read and the defendant offered his plea.

"On the charge of murder in the first degree of Sandra French, how do you plead?" asked the clerk.

"Not guilty," said Francois in a monotone.

"On the charge of murder in the first degree of Wendy Meyers, how do you plead?"

"Not guilty."

"On the charge of murder in the first degree of Kathleen Hurley, how do you plead?"

"Not guilty."

"On the charge of murder in the first degree of Catina Newmaster, how do you plead?"

"Not guilty."

"On the charge of murder in the first degree of Gina Barone, how do you plead?"

"Not guilty."

"On the charge of murder in the first degree of Audrey Pugliese, how do you plead?"

"Not guilty."

"On the charge of murder in the first degree of Catherine Marsh, how do you plead?"

"Not guilty."

"On the charge of murder in the first degree of Mary Giaccone, how do you plead?"

"Not guilty."

And so it went until the rest of the charges were read and pleaded to. At the prosecution's table, Assistant District Attorney William O'Neill remained impassive. Grady wasn't prosecuting the case, but O'Neill, the DA's good right hand, was implementing Grady's prosecution strategy.

Grady wasn't tipping his hand. Yet. No one knew if he would seek death. He had 120 days from the day of the arraignment, until the middle of February 1999, to make that decision.

With the charges read and answered, the proceeding was over. But as Francois was being led out of the courtroom, the relatives began taunting him again. Francois threw his head back, smiled and chuckled to himself. It was a strange reaction from a man facing death.

Francois had refused all requests for interviews. It was hard to know what was going on inside his warped head. But as he shuffled out of the courtroom, more than one observer could be heard muttering something to the effect of not wanting to ever encounter the big fellow in a dark alley. That dark alleys were not part of his MO made no difference.

In his brief appearance in court, Kendall Francois had managed to live up to his billing. He actually looked like what the media had portrayed him to be—big, powerful, unyielding, with a derisive ghostly laugh that left the final, lasting impression that this was indeed the bogeyman of nightmares.

Sixteen

It was time to cut bait.

Treece knew the DA had him over a barrel. Despite public pronouncements, Francois's guilt was immutable, his conviction on murder one almost assured. Rather than take the chance of a jury giving him death, Treece contacted Grady and tried to work out a deal.

He'd save the state the cost of a trial and an execution. Francois would plead guilty. In return, his sentence would be life in prison without parole. Treece went into court and tried pleading guilty on behalf of his client, in return for a life sentence. Grady quickly rejected the deal. Treece said he would appeal. It was an interesting case.

Intellectually, observers had to wonder whether the state had to take the plea. Or were they free to continue and seek the death penalty? A lot depended on the pulse of the community that Grady served.

Many times, prosecutors want to shoot the moon while their constituents just want closure. In the Francois case, it was pretty evenly divided, not just by the voting public, but by the people closest to the case, the families of the dead women. Some wanted the case disposed of as soon as possible; life in prison was enough for the bastard. Others clung to a burning hope that the state would shoot poison into his veins and Francois would die in agony.

Christmas Eve, 1998

He was Santa Claus. It would come as a tremendous shock to Tawana Brawley and the many people Grady had associated with professionally over the years that the prosecutor would have been looked at this way.

"I called him [Grady] this morning and said I wanted an early Christmas present. I think I got it. They called me back and said, 'Merry Christmas, you are getting your Christmas gift,' " said Heidi Cramer, to a local paper.

"It really surprised me. The day before Christmas. Never in a million years," said Treece.

"This is the first Christmas without my mother and by next Christmas I want him dead. I know it may sound cold and heartless; I know Christmastime you're supposed to be forgiving, but guess what? I ain't," Cramer continued. "There is a Santa Claus and today his name is William Grady."

Their "present" was Grady's surprise announcement on Christmas Eve. At two P.M., Bill Grady announced that he would seek the death penalty against Kendall Francois. Had it been any other day of the year, no death penalty opponent, of which there were many in the state, would have thought of Grady as a modern-day Pontius Pilate, the Roman prelate who had condemned Jesus to the cross. But being that it was Christmas Eve, the historical metaphor was inescapable.

Francois, though, was no savior, and Grady was certainly not an evil person like Pilate. In the end, it came down to a cold, hard, political reality. If the DA could get a jury to unanimously agree, Kendall Francois was going to the death chamber. The popular perception was that Treece's aggressiveness in representing his client had forced Grady's hand, a charge Treece rejected.

"We represent our client and that's what we are going to do. We are going to give him zealous representation," he said. "By representing our client we forced this? I don't think so," said Treece in the *Times Herald Record*.

Patricia Barone, though, wasn't convinced.

"The timing stinks, but what are you going to do?" Barone said. "The Capital Defender Office wants to play games around Christmas. They have no conscience as far as I'm concerned."

Not true. The defense hadn't forced Grady's hand, or the law. He still had until February to file for death. Treece's attempt to plead had provided Grady with the kind of political cover that might even win over death penalty opponents.

"I had two Christmases of wondering where she was, so this Christmas is a little more peaceful. Now he gets to suffer through the holidays knowing that there's the possibility he's going to die. Now I'm so happy," said Heidi Cramer.

Treece was still determined to get the DA to accept a plea. He filed a brief with a county court judge, using as precedent a court of appeals ruling in another death penalty case in which the court opened the door to such pleas in death penalty cases. Treece's legal argument was promptly rejected. He then filed an expedited brief before the state court of appeals. Maybe they would see things Francois's way.

In the meantime, it was now his job to travel down from his Albany office to the Poughkeepsie jail and let Francois know that a lethal injection loomed on his horizon.

A year went by and nothing happened, but there is nothing terribly unusual about that. It takes a while for a case before the court of appeals to get a docket number and then be presented and then have the opinion written and published. Back in Poughkeepsie, everyone was on edge waiting to see what would happen. Over on Fulton Avenue, progress was being made. Someone had actually found a way to make a profit out of the whole mess.

The Francois home had been bought by a real estate entrepreneur. The Francois family had been forced to sell because there was no way they could go back there. The worst thing that could happen to the value of your property is that you are the family of a serial killer. That's a guarantee right there that the price is going to go down.

It didn't just go down. It plummeted.

The Francois home in the best of markets could easily sell for close to $200,000. Instead, it sold for $15,000. The person who bought it then gutted the interior and completely redid it. Suddenly, the beautiful wood interior of the house was restored to its Victorian glory. Empty, ready for sale, the place looked positively pristine.

The floors inside were waxed and glowing. Attention had been paid to the painting so even the moldings were carefully done. The stairs in the house seemed to lead up to what looked like a very attractive series of upstairs bedrooms. Best of all, the place smelled great. Up in the attic, the only thing you could smell was . . . an attic. Nothing special. Just the way any attic in America smells.

"I want the house down. It's just a lousy, lousy feeling for me. I want it down, the land cleared and blessed because the place was truly a tomb for eight women," Pat Barone, Gina's mother told the *Poughkeepsie Journal*, in response to news that the place was going to be sold and once again inhabited.

May 19, 2000

By a vote of seven to none, the New York State Court of Appeals rejected Treece's arguments that the state had to accept Francois's plea and sided with Grady.

Deciding otherwise would lead to an "unseemly race to the courthouse between defense and prosecution to see whether a guilty plea or notice of intent to seek the death penalty will be filed first," wrote Appeals Judge Harold Levine. Levine called that the direct opposite of "thorough, fully deliberative decision-making" that the court believed prosecutors should go through when seeking death.

"This decision in essence closes the door with regard to any future attempts by defendants to enter pleas in advance of either the 120-day period running or the district attorney filing his death notice," said a triumphant Grady.

If nothing else, Grady was making Francois sweat. Grady may not have been a brilliant lawyer, but he was a good one. He knew how to read evidence and state statutes. Sure, he was convinced that under the legal definition of sanity, the ability to know right from wrong, that Francois was sane at the time of the murders.

But the DA also knew from examining Francois's probation report, which the state did not make and has never made public, that there were certain psychiatric factors in his background that might make it difficult to get a jury to agree to death. Grady knew that the defense could effectively show mitigating factors during the penalty phase of the trial.

Put another way, all the defense had to show

was that Francois was psychotic and the jury
would have no choice but to spare his life.

Then there was the practical consideration.
The trial would be long. So would the appeals
process; that could take five years. Grady really
didn't want to make a deal. He really wanted
the guy to pay for his crime. He also wanted
to be sure of a win and one never knew what
a jury would decide.

It has become common practice in today's
world of jurisprudence for the district attorney,
regardless of venue, to consult with the victims'
relatives in cutting a deal. The idea is to get
the families to sign off on it so that they feel
justice is done and at the same time the DA is
guaranteed a conviction.

Grady contacted the families of the eight and
told them what he had in mind.

June 22, 2000

In Judge Dolan's courtroom, the same one
in which Kendall Francois had been arraigned,
there were approximately 150 filling the pews.
The place was packed and the majority were
friends and relatives of the victims.

Francois stood at his place at the defense table and shuffled forward with his lawyers.
Knowing that he would be doing just that at
the hearing had made the court take certain
precautions.

Three armed sheriff's deputies from the
Dutchess County Sheriff's Office bunched in so

tightly around him, they were touching. Four more armed deputies stood guard at the door leading into Judge Dolan's courtroom. Dolan sat on the bench and looked down at Francois, the hulking defendant at the bar. Dolan himself had three court officers armed with automatics at the waist stationed around him.

Shuffling up to the bar was the object of all this attention, Kendall L. Francois, bogeyman incarnate. Once again he was shackled and dressed in prison orange. Only this time, Francois had a few things to say, though Grady had made the right decision to avoid details.

When defendants take a plea in a major felony, they are usually required to go through a public recitation of the details of the crime so that, on one hand, the court record shows that the defendant gave details of the crime he has pled to and, on the other, that the families of the decedents get the satisfaction of seeing their loved ones' killer take responsibility for his crime in a court of law.

For Francois, it was really a coming-out party of sorts. He had worked hard in Richard Reitano's government studies course at Dutchess County Community College. He was now getting an opportunity to see how things worked in the real world, not the safe, clean academic one.

Francois knew going into court that he was going to jail for the rest of his life. He knew that everyone looked at him as some kind of animal. How could he not? He read the same papers in prison that people read outside, including the *New York Times*. He saw the same shows on CNN. He knew that any hearings from now on would be reported nationally. And he acted accordingly and, strangely, with dignity.

Francois fell back on the one thing in his life that had given him discipline—his training as a soldier in the army. When he responded to the judge's questions, it was like a soldier taking responsibility for his actions.

"Did you kill Wendy Meyers?" Judge Dolan began.

"Yes, sir," Francois answered.

"Did you kill Gina Barone?"

"Guilty."

"Did you kill Sandra French?"

"Yes, sir, I did."

"Did you kill Audrey Pugliese?"

"Yes, sir."

"Did you kill Kathleen Hurley?"

"Guilty."

"Did you kill Catina Newmaster?"

"Yes, sir."

A woman in the family section behind the district attorney's side of the courtroom began to cry. Her name was Barbara Perry. Held tight to her bosom was an eight-by-ten photograph of her daughter. Barbara was Catina Newmaster's mother. She remembered the little Catina, whom Bill Siegrist had befriended.

"Did you kill Mary Hcaley Giaccone?"

"Yes, sir."

"Did you kill Catherine Marsh?"

"Guilty."

"Did you assault Diane Franco at your home?"

"Guilty."

There was a pause and then the judge turned to Bill Grady. The district attorney himself was in the courtroom representing his county.

"I understand that the state wishes to inquire?"

"Yes, Your Honor."

Grady had a question.

"Did anyone else help you commit these murders?"

Francois knew it was coming.

"No, sir. My family had nothing to do with any of this."

In a way, it was a gift from Grady to the Francois family. In one fell swoop, he had alleviated any public doubt that might exist, and there was a lot of it, that they had had some complicity in the crimes. In open court, Grady absolved them of any legal responsibility in the deaths of the eight.

The homicide survivors, the friends and relatives of the slain women, had listened in their section of the courtroom. To them, it was like attending a funeral. Some sobbed more quietly than Perry had. Others remained impassive, and still others looked toward the ceiling, as if to heaven, to see the deceased once again, or perhaps to let out a silent prayer that justice was finally being done and they could rest in peace.

Before the proceedings finished, Mark Harris, of the Capital Defender Office, told the court that Francois was HIV positive. His illegal activities had resulted in his contracting a disease for which there was no known cure.

After the hearing, Grady told reporters:

"How the victims' families felt about the disposition, although not controlling, was an important factor in deciding to accept this plea. . . . We were absolutely convinced that we could obtain a guilty verdict . . . but we were of the opinion we could not overcome [the psychiatric issues]. This disposition represents the only realistic way to hold the defendant fully accountable for his heinous crimes and ensure closure for the families."

For his part, Capital Defender Harris stated that life imprisonment was "a just resolution" and that while Francois would live, "his life will be spared, but he will answer for his actions."

Paulette Francois publicly became the family spokesperson. Through her attorney, Marco Caviglia, she released a statement that said she had the "greatest sympathy" for the families of the victims. "We know their sorrow firsthand as this ordeal has caused us to lose our beloved McKinley, husband and father, whose broken heart finally yielded," she said in the statement.

It was . . . interesting. Paulette Francois was comparing the loss of her husband, by the seemingly natural cause of a broken heart, to families who had lost their loved ones due to her son's murderous rages.

One of the homicide victims' survivors felt for the Francois family. It was Heidi Cramer. Cramer recalled when her mother had shot a man when she was twelve years old. She remembered the stigma involved with that crime that she had to endure. It was the same type of stigma the Francoises would now have to live with as the family of a serial killer.

August 8, 2000

Another trend in jurisprudence is victim impact statements. Before a defendant is sentenced, the families of the victims are allowed to address the defendant directly, in open court, and tell the defendant how his actions have affected their lives. That would happen on a summer day, a sweltering one in Judge Dolan's courtroom.

The armed officers were there, ten in all, three around Francois. Francois was seated at the defense table, once again shackled and in his orange jail clothing. He wore glasses and his hair was close cropped. Judge Dolan turned the proceedings over to the families. Throughout the testimonies, Francois would keep looking down, never up, never meeting the survivors' eyes, no matter what they said. He was acting as though he had a conscience.

One by one, they walked to the lectern directly opposite Francois and were allowed to directly address him. One by one, the victims' family members came to the lectern. It made no difference who said what. The pain was the same.

"I never fully understood the impact of

wakes until today because she was a skeleton when they found her."

"You deserve to die, Kendall. There is no way I believe your family didn't have something to do with what happened."

"Those of you who knew her well surely will agree that he killed her and took her away from us. We will never have the chance to hear her laugh or see her girlish smile. When she was a child, she used to ask, 'Will the monsters get me?' What you did to her and the other women was unspeakable and unforgettable. These terrible acts of murder will never be forgiven. I hope he suffers to the last breath. AIDS will certainly kill him if prison doesn't."

"He should be executed eight times, once for each life he took. If anyone must refer to them in any way, refer to them as women," a clear allusion to the constant dehumanization of the victims in the press, which always referred to them as the "eight prostitutes," not eight women.

"At any point, did any of them beg for mercy? It breaks our heart knowing you were the last person she ever saw."

The relatives, sitting in eight rows on the side of the courtroom behind the DA, applauded.

"We know someday you'll die from this [AIDS]. It seems like poetic justice, isn't it, Kendall? It will kill the man who killed our mother. You took away a very wonderful woman. Our family hopes you rot in hell."

"She was born March 3, 1967. It often felt like she was our only child. She was well adjusted. She was raised in a loving, Christian home. Her father died of a heart attack at the age of ten. She played softball, basketball and started using alcohol and cocaine to numb her feelings. She was at Geneseo for one month [before she started] experimenting with drugs. Her disease raged on [as she] became a cocaine addict.

"[She] loved her daughters. She entered [a rehab facility] in Saranac Lake and while she was there worked hard for sobriety. [Then] she entered the halfway house in Poughkeepsie. She was attending Dutchess County Community College. She was going to get a degree in human services. But the only housing she could get was in the heart of the drug district.

"She struggled to attend school. She wanted to get her kids back and then relapsed. She [had] lost her children, her car, clothes. By November 1996, she was back on the street. [Still] she had made plans to come home and go into rehabilitation [again]. She died before her thirtieth birthday.

"She was the victim of a terrible disease that Mr. Francois preyed on. To you, Mr. Francois, in one brief instance, you snuffed out a life and desecrated her body. You took the life of the child she was carrying within her. I will never again be able to kneel next to her at Mass. I will never again be able to play backgammon or Scrabble with her. There will always be an empty chair, someone missing at dinners. Mr. Francois, you took all that away in one split second.

"I will not pass judgment on you. 'Vengeance is mine, sayeth the Lord.' "

When it was over, the judge looked down and addressed the courtroom.

"All of you have been affected by this tragedy," he said sympathetically. "Mr. Harris, come forward."

Francois and his attorney, Mark Harris, came before the bar for sentencing.

"Mr. Francois wishes to tell the court that he is deeply sorry and regrets the pain and sorrow he caused," said Harris.

"Yes, sir," Francois added.

"At the time the plea was entered," said the judge, "I commended both sides for [seeing] the utter futility of a trial. This result is just."

Dolan turned his steely gaze on the serial murderer.

"Mr. Francois, there is very little I can say here. Their anger and loss is so real. It is felt in this courtroom and community. You and you alone are responsible for this vicious and unspeakable violence. [These] acts recoil through the community in horror and anger." While Francois killed, the community "didn't have freedom from fear." Dolan was hopeful that his sentencing would be a "final resolution to this case.

"On the charge of murder in the first degree of Audrey Pugliese, the sentence is twenty-five years to life.

"On the charge of murder in the first degree of Sandra French, the sentence is twenty-five years to life.

"On the charge of murder in the first degree of Mary Giaccone, the sentence is twenty-five years to life.

"On the charge of murder in the first degree of Kathleen Hurley, the sentence is twenty-five years to life.

"On the charge of murder in the first degree of Catherine Marsh, the sentence is twenty-five years to life.

"On the charge of murder in the first degree of Gina Barone, the sentence is twenty-five years to life.

"On the charge of murder in the first degree of Wendy Meyers, the sentence is twenty-five years to life.

"On the charge of murder in the first degree of Catina Newmaster, the sentence is twenty-five years to life. The intention of the court is for the sentences to be served consecutively."

In other words, Kendall Francois would have to serve a minimum of two hundred years in prison before he could even be considered rehabilitated.

"On the charge of the attempted second-degree assault of Diane Franco, the sentence is one and a half to three years."

That sentence, of course, didn't matter. It was a simple matter of justice for Franco. However, in any sentencing, even of a serial killer, there is a certain formality to the hearing that requires the judge to ask the defendant several questions.

"Has the clerk advised you of your right to appeal?"

"Yes, sir," Francois answered.

Francois also acknowledged in court that as part of his plea agreement, he had given up his right to appeal his sentence.

"Yes, sir," Francois answered again, though in actuality there was one automatic appeal that had to be sent in. In capital cases, the defense lawyers always file a motion that they themselves did not provide adequate counsel to the defendant, hoping for the long shot that the court of appeals will buy that argument and give them a new trial. That remote possibility could then result in a further lessening of the sentence.

The court would reject that subsequent appeal. Francois's sentence would, of course, stand.

"Mr. Francois, you are remanded to the state correctional system."

He was marched away by the deputies, one husky one on each arm. They hustled him out of the well of the courtroom and through a side door. For just a second, while the deputies cleared the path down an interior corridor, Francois stood in the doorway alone.

His back was massive. The baby fat that covered him was, like everything else about him, deceiving. It was mostly muscle, converted into strength that gave him a cruel weapon against everyone who had ever made fun of him because of his size. The doorway seemed to grow smaller with him standing there.

At last, the deputies pulled him inside the corridor and Kendall Francois, for the last time, vanished from view.

EPILOGUE

Neither police nor prosecutor ever gave a reason for why Kendall L. Francois killed the eight women. They didn't have to, nor were they obligated to under the law.

When police have as strong a case as Siegrist and company did against Francois, there is no necessity to probe for motive. They probe for motive when they need it for a conviction, which in this case was never really in doubt.

As far as the cops are concerned, it's up to the sociologists and the psychologists to find the reasons why. They really don't care. If they did, they couldn't do their jobs. There are too many bad guys out there. Motive is a luxury. Their job is to catch 'em.

Likewise, the prosecutor does not need to prove motive to get a conviction. While motive, means and opportunity are the triumvirate of the criminal prosecution process, having a confession, bodies and other forensic evidence tying the killer to the victims is usually enough for any jury to convict without having motive.

But that still doesn't answer the question burning in the minds of most people who studied this case: why did Kendall Francois kill eight women? What blood lust did he satisfy?

There were intimations from various sources in the writing of this book that there was a sexual component behind the crimes. That certainly made sense, considering his choice of victims. But what weird sexual urge Francois might have satisfied remains itself a mystery.

Seeking to resolve these questions, I wrote Kendall Francois at his prison cell in Attica State Prison in upstate New York where he currently resides. He never answered my letters.

The Francois family have drawn a complete circle of silence around themselves. To date, they have not talked about his motive to the press, or anything else, for that matter. They just want the public to forget the whole thing and let them live in peace. That might be hard.

Police suspect, and I concur, that Francois committed more murders. Seeking that route, I contacted the Department of the Army, U.S. Army Personnel Command in St. Louis, Missouri. A request was made for access to Francois's military record under the United States Freedom of Information Act. Every citizen is entitled to look at it. The idea was to see if there was anything in Francois's service record that might have indicated a predilection for this kind of violence. That could also show that the office of the Judge Advocate General had investigated anything, from some sort of disturbed, erratic behavior to actual allegations of sexual violence. After repeated vague army replies dated January 10 and March 29, 2000, the last one I received, dated June 6, says the following:

"Every reasonable effort is being made to locate the records needed to reply to your inquiry. Your patience is greatly appreciated."

The letter is signed "Peggy Barton, Case Analyst." That was two years ago! And still they have not responded.

Might there be something *really* interesting in Francois's military record?

When I began writing true crime books nine years ago, I always probed for motive. I figured the answers always lay in the killers' background, especially their childhood. In my naïveté, I always assumed a Freudian reason for the crime.

As I became more experienced as an investigator, I began to realize that it isn't as cut and dried as all that. For every person abused as a child who becomes a killer, I could show you thousands who go on to lead worthwhile, productive lives.

Scientists are still trying to figure out if there's a "murder" gene and who has it. In Francois's case, I suspect his crimes were rooted in some childhood psychosis, plus a genetic factor. But one intriguing question that can be answered is this:

Why did Kendall Francois bathe the bodies? For the answer, I turned to investigative psychologist Dr. Maurice Godwin.

"Another way in which police attempt to deduce what occurred in a series of murders is to record those actions that are unique across the offense series," he writes in his book *Criminal Psychology and Forensic Technology*.

For example, the unique behaviors that serial murderers repeatedly leave at their crime scenes are referred to, in the realms of forensic and criminal investigations, as the killer's "psychological signature." These unique patterns of behaviors have been explained by the FBI as traits, and they claim that the person variable repeatedly shows consistency across crimes. However . . . there lies danger in using the term "trait" as a cause of behavior.

To say that an offender left the victim nude after the murder explains nothing. Ressler [the famous FBI criminologist] and his colleagues argue that signature actions are revealed due to the offender acting out in fulfillment of his violent fantasies.

According to Ressler and his colleagues, fantasy may be manifested through particular verbal interaction with the victim, or through committing a series of actions on the victim in a particular order. However, an offender's M.O. or signature is not always present in every murder due to agencies, such as disturbances during the course of an offense or an unanticipated victim response, or because the body of the victim has decomposed prior to its discovery; therefore the signature aspect has been destroyed.

But in Francois's case, his signature behavior, bathing the bodies, is known because he said he did it. No deduction is needed. Godwin goes on to define signature behavior as:

. . . types of extraordinary violence similarities.

For example, the victim was beaten beyond the point needed to kill her, or the killer seemed preoccupied with the victim's clothing or took some time to pose the victim's body . . . in leaving his signature, a killer's psychodrama is evolving. Although the scene is different, the act contained the same plot, same characters, and same dialogue which came to the same conclusion.

Francois's bathing of the bodies was his distinctive signature behavior. Why did he do it? As Godwin cautions, more information would be necessary for a detailed analysis. But one possibility is that by bathing them, he was making the women, whom he clearly saw as impure, pure again in death.

However, determining the underlying structure of offenders' signature behaviors requires extensive empirical analysis beyond any that is currently in use by police forces. By identifying the combinations of behavioral variables and background characteristics, which accounts for an offender's individuality, is the most logical way forward in order to facilitate an understanding of consistency and development in offending behavior through time.

Understanding your quarry, as any hunter will tell you, is essential to the tracking process. Law enforcement's continued reliance on the outmoded, ineffectual and unproven FBI serial killer organized and disorganized modality does nothing to help in catching these criminals. Had the FBI been able to provide real quality guidance, the kind Godwin is referring to, the investigation might have quickened.

Godwin also has a few things to say about the way the crime is committed by the serial killer.

The traditional use of Modus Operandi (M.O.), as a basis for linking offenses, is premised on the investigator's deductive reasoning that the M.O. is static and uniquely characteristic to a particular offender. For example, traditionally M.O. is defined as distinctive actions, which link crimes together. As evidenced by this definition, many times the investigators confuse the offender's M.O. with his signature, as if the two were the same.

In the Francois case, the investigators concentrated on neither. They were just too overwhelmed in catching the guy. Godwin continues:

An M.O. accounts for the type of crime and property used to commit a crime. The offender's M.O. includes the victim type, the time and place the crime was committed, the tools or implements used, the way the criminal gained entry or how he approached or subdued his victim, including disguises or uniforms, and ways he represented himself to a victim.

Clearly, Francois's M.O. was the type of victim he chose, always consistent; choosing to kill with his hands, always consistent; and where he picked them up, again always consistent. He never deviated, which is why the police's hope that he was responsible for Eason's death is just that, hope, and not based on scientific fact.

Eason's only relationship to the other victims was that she, too, was a prostitute. She was, however, African American. If Francois had suddenly decided to target African Americans, why weren't more of the victims black?

An offender's M.O. can and does change over time as he discovers that some things can be done more effectively. The M.O. of a killer is only those actions which are necessary to commit the murder. However, using M.O. to classify or link crime scene behavior is rather unreliable as it does not take into account the many offense dynamics which can affect an offender's change in behavior due to such influences as changing victim reaction from offense to offense.

The offender's M.O. can change over time as a result of a number of factors, such as experience, which when committing crimes such as rape or murder, leads to refinements or changes in his conduct so as to facilitate the completion of the crime. These refinements in criminal actions can have a number of causes, for example, the result of being arrested or, as a result of victim response, causing the offender to change his way of dealing with the victim, including any future victims.

Note that Francois's murder of Audrey Pugliese differed from the other victims: he stomped her viciously, but only after his arrest and incarceration on the misdemeanor assault charge. Eason's disappearance, however, occurred before his arrest.

"The change in behavior could be attributed to factors, such as maintaining control over the victim by the use of a weapon or, for example, a rapist progressing to murder in order to avoid identification."

In Pugliese's murder, Francois was clearly punishing her for trying to escape from him. He knew he didn't have to use his feet to kill her; his hands, used repeatedly in the past, would have been up to the task. Yet none of this can truly explain the enormity of Kendall

Francois's crimes. I've lived with them for the past two years it has taken to put this story together. My informed conclusion is this:

Kendall L. Francois is evil, pure evil, and he is where he belongs, behind bars, where he can no longer create tragedy. What do you think?

Fred Rosen can be reached at crimedoesntpay.com

Acknowledgments

This book could not have been written without the cooperation of three men who, between them, lived every minute of this case—Bill Siegrist, Jimmy Ayling and Tommy Martin. It was Jimmy who first clued me into what was really going on and provided entry into the law enforcement apparatus that was utilized in catching the killer.

Bill gave generously of his time to sit for interviews by the Hudson River. With painstaking honesty, he described every facet of the investigation, including what he perceived as his foibles and what I perceive as his humanity. It is the kind of unprecedented access every writer hopes for and rarely gets.

Tommy Martin not only told me, but showed me, how he and Kevin Rosa worked the crime scene. It's a far cry from what you see on television, and that much more fascinating.

Jim DeFelice gave generously of his time and cigars when explaining to me the ins and outs of Poughkeepsie and Dutchess County.

Paul Dinas, the former editor-in-chief of Kensington Books, deserves credit for seeing the commercial possibility in this story and the fact that readers would want to know what really happened. Karen Haas, my former consulting editor, helped me make this a better book.

I hope that in some way I have managed to bring some humanity to the lives of the women who were so maligned in the press as nothing more than prostitutes and drug users. Their deaths will have an impact on their sons and daughters, their mothers and fathers, for the rest of their lives and, in the case of the children, into future generations. It is my hope for all of them that they move on.

While the type of revenge fantasies that were evident at the sentencing are normal for the victims' families, what I have seen in the numerous murder cases I have investigated is that those who adjust best are those who actually forgive the murderer and move on. All revenge will do is corrode from the inside out.

There are worse things than a quick death by needle, including, I believe, confinement to a cell for the rest of your natural life. Every time Kendall Francois feels like killing someone and can't, and turns those emotions inside out, the eight women will be getting their revenge.

An old Sicilian proverb says it best:

"Revenge is a dish best eaten cold."

—Fred Rosen
April, 2002

Appendix

KENDALL FRANCOIS AS LEGAL PRECEDENT

The precedent that the New York State Court of Appeals set in the Kendall Francois case may very well be the defining piece of law when it comes to pleas in cases regarding serial killers.

What the New York State Court of Appeals said in the matter of law was that a capital defender representing a serial killer might not cop to a lesser plea before the district attorney has even had the opportunity to ask for death. The New York state courts' opinions are frequently used as precedents in other states looking for guidance in this area of jurisprudence.

What the court of appeals said is best read in their own words. Here is the actual text of their decision.

2 No. 46

In the Matter of Kendall Francois, Appellant,

v.

Thomas J. Dolan, &c., et al., Respondents.

2000 NY Int. 64
May 18, 2000

Barry Fisher, for appellant.
Bridget Rahilly Steller, for respondent District Attorney.

LEVINE, J.:
  The issue in this case is whether mandamus lies to compel County Court to entertain petititoner's offer to plead guilty to all counts of the indictment charging him with capital mur-

der, before the filing by the District Attorney
of a notice of intent to seek the death penalty
and prior to the expiration of the statutory period within which such notice may be filed. We
agree with the Appellate Division that mandamus does not lie in this case because petitioner
had no unqualified statutory right, let alone
the required "clear legal right" for mandamus,
to plead guilty under these circumstances.

On October 8, 1998, a Dutchess County
Grand Jury indicted petitioner Kendall Francois
on eight counts of murder in the first degree,
as defined under New York's 1995 death penalty
legislation (*see, Penal Law § 125.27*[1][a][xi]; L
1995, ch 1), eight counts of murder in the second degree (*Penal Law § 125.25*[1]) and one
count of attempted second degree assault (*Penal
Law §§ 110.00* and 120.05[1]). He was arraigned
on the indictment and entered a plea of not
guilty. Pursuant to CPL 250.40(2), Francois' arraignment marked the beginning of a 120-day
period within which the District Attorney was
authorized to serve a notice of intent to seek
the death penalty. In November, the District Attorney wrote to the Capital Defender Office in-
viting the submission of any mitigation
information the defense might request the
prosecutor to consider in determining whether
to seek the death penalty.

On December 22, 1998, before the District
Attorney either filed a notice of intent to seek
the death penalty or announced his intention
not to do so, this Court decided *Matter of Hynes*
v *Tomei* (, *92 NY2d 613, cert denied* __US__).

There we considered a challenge, under *United States* v *Jackson* (*390 US 570*), to the constitutionality of the 1995 death penalty statute. As we explained in *Hynes,* the specific defect the Supreme Court identified in the Federal Kidnaping Act was that it "authorized the death penalty only on the recommendation of a jury, while a defendant *convicted of the same offense* on a guilty plea or by a Judge escaped the threat of capital punishment" (*id.,* at 621 [citing *United States* v *Jackson, supra,* at 583] [emphasis supplied]), thus needlessly burdening an accused's Fifth and *Sixth Amendment* rights.

We held in *Matter of Hynes* v *Tomei* that this State's capital punishment statue had a *Jackson* infirmity. We described the statutory scheme under which, when the District Attorney elects to seek the death penalty, a jury trial is provided for the guilt-adjudication stage and then, upon conviction, there is a mandated second "sentencing proceeding before a jury to determine whether the penalty imposed will be death or life imprisonment without parole (*see,* CPL 400.27)" (*id.,* at 622). However, the statute permitted a guilty plea to first degree murder only "with both the permission of the court and the consent of the people *when the agreed upon sentence* is either *life imprisonment without parole or a term of imprisonment* for the Class A-I felony or murder in the first degree" (CPL 220.10[5][e]; 220.30[3][b][vii] [emphasis supplied]). Thus, we concluded in *Matter of Hynes* v *Tomei* that, just as under the Federal Kidnaping Act struck down in *United States* v *Jackson,* avoidance of the maximum penalty for conviction of the capital offense (here, murder in the first degree) could only be assured to defendants who plead guilty rather than assert innocence and go to trial before a jury.

Instead of invalidating the entire statute in *Hynes*, however, we held that the death penalty legislation could be saved from this particular challenge by severance of the offending guilty plea provisions contained in CPL 220.10(5)(e) and 220.30(3)(b)(vii). We, therefore, limited our ruling to declaring those specific sections unconstitutional and striking them from the statute. Because the District Attorney had already filed a notice of intent to seek the death penalty (*see, id.,* 237 AD2d 52, 54), we also interpreted the statute as prohibiting a guilty plea to capital murder while such a death penalty notice was pending (*see, id.,* 92 NY2d, at 629).

On December 23, the day following the decision in *Matter of Hynes* v *Tomei,* still before a death penalty notice had been filed by the District Attorney in this case, petitioner made an uncalendared appearance before County Court, Dutchess County, in which he offered to plead guilty to the entire indictment. The District Attorney opposed acceptance of the plea and, the following day, filed the death penalty notice. County Court reserved decision on the guilty plea offer and later rendered a decision refusing to accept the plea.

Petitioner then brought before the Appellate Division the instant CPLR article 78 proceeding, in the nature of mandamus, for an order directing County Court to "entertain" his plea of guilty to the entire indictment. The Appellate Division dismissed the petition, holding that mandamus did not lie here because petitioner "failed to demonstrate a legal right to the relief sought" (__AD2d__,__). We agree. The legislative scheme does not support the theory that a person indicted for capital murder has an unqualified right, by pleading guilty to the indictment, to thwart the statutory authority of a District Attorney to make a fully deliberative decision whether to seek the death penalty, within the 120-day period after arraignment prescribed by CPL2.

Petitioner's case for mandamus, requiring the trial court to entertain his guilty plea to the entire indictment, rests on CPL 220.10(2) and 220.60(2), general plea of provisions of the Criminal Procedure Law. Petitioner argues that these sections, which were enacted before, and left in place by, the death penalty statute, in the absence of the stricken provisions, give all defendants, including those charged with capital murder, an absolute right to plead guilty to an entire indictment upon arraignment and at any time before verdict.

For several reasons we reject this argument and hold that until the completion of the statutorily provided deliberative process, either by the filing of a death penalty notice, announcement of an intention not to seek that sanction, or by the expiration of the statutory period to make that decision, a capital defendant does not have an unqualified right to plead guilty to the entire indictment. Thus, to the extent that there is a conflict between sections 220.10(2) and 220.60(2), on the one hand, and the provision giving the District Attorney the authority to decide whether to seek the death penalty and a period to deliberate on that decision (*see,* CPL 250.40), the latter provision prevails.

Of foremost importance, if as petitioner contends, he has an unqualified right to plead guilty to an entire capital crime indictment, two critical powers conferred on the District Attorney in the 1995 death penalty legislation could be preempted. First, the defendant could thereby prevent the prosecution from pursuing the death penalty even *after* a notice of intent to seek the death penalty was filed under CPL 250.40(1). This is because there is no provision for impaneling a jury for the required death penalty sentencing stage after a guilty plea to capital murder (*see,* CPL 400.27; *Matter of Hynes* v *Tomei,* 92 NY2d, at 629 n 7). Thus, the only legal sentence upon a guilty plea would be either life imprisonment without parole or a term of years in prison. In order to avoid this result, in *Matter of Hynes* v *Tomei,* we construed the statute, as a whole, not to permit a capital defendant to exercise an unqualified right to plead guilty to murder in the first degree while a death penalty notice was pending (*see, Matter of Hynes* v *Tomei, supra,* 92 NY2d, at 629).

Second, in entering a plea to capital murder, a defendant could preclude the District Attorney from even exercising the statutory right to consider, over time (weighing aggravating and mitigating factors), whether to seek the ultimate sanction in a capital murder case. This implication is presented here, and would be the end result of acceptance of petitioner's position on this appeal. The statutory structure and the legislative history show that the role of the District Attorney, and attendant statutory rights and responsibilities, was the keystone of the 1995 bill. The prosecutor's filing of a notice of intent to seek the death penalty is a *sine qua non* for the imposition of the ultimate sanction in a capital case (*see*, CPL 250.40[1] ["A sentence of death *may not* be imposed * * * unless * * * the people file * * * and serve * * * a notice of intent to seek the death penalty"]). That prosecutorial authority and the statutory time frame for its exercise are emphasized as a central feature of the bill in the Governor's Program Bill Memorandum (Bill Jacket, L 1995, ch 1, at 14), as well as in the Assembly Codes Committee Memorandum (*id.*, at 23). Conversely, when sections 220.10(2) and 210.60(2), relied upon here by petitioner, were originally enacted, the Legislature expressly evinced its intention to limit their application in capital cases under the death penalty statute of that time (*see*, CPL former 220.10[5][e]; 220.60[1]; Preiser, Practice Commentaries, McKinney's Cons Laws of NY, Book 11A, CPL 220.10, at 11). Thus, petitioner's proposed interpretation would substantially undermine the present statutory framework, and is not supported by the legislative history of those provisions.

Moreover, giving precedence to the subsequently enacted, specific provision of section 250.40 over the earlier enacted, more general provisions of CPL 220.10(2) and 220.60(2) is consistent with the canon of statutory interpretation most directly applicable here: "what is special or particular in the later of two statues supersedes as an exception whatever in the earlier statute is unlimited or general" (*East End Trust Co.* v *Otten,* 255 NY 283, 286 [Cardozo, CH. J.]; *see, Gwynne* v *Board of Educ.,* 259 NY 191, 197).

Finally, we should not ignore the unintended and untoward effects of a contrary ruling. As this case illustrates, and County Court pointed out, it would inevitably result, in the most heinous or high profile cases, in an unseemly race to the courthouse between defense and prosecution to see whether a guilty plea or notice of intent to seek the death penalty will be filed first. The need for precipitous action to file a death penalty notice before the plea was offered would undeniably preclude the thorough, fully deliberative decision-making on whether to seek the death penalty that the Legislature contemplated, and one would hope a District Attorney would employ, in the exercise of that official's profound responsibilities conferred under the present death penalty statute. For all of these reasons, we hold that the Appellate Division properly dismissed the petition here.

Accordingly, the judgment of the Appellate Division should be affirmed, without costs.

Judgment affirmed, without costs. Opinion

by Judge Levine. Chief Judge Kaye and Judges Bellacosa, Smith, Ciparick, Wesley and Rosenblatt concur.
    Decided May 18, 2000